Captain Cook

IN CLEVELAND

Painted by N. Dance Esq. R.A.   Engraved by W. Holl.

CAPTAIN JAMES COOK.

IN CLEVELAND

CLIFF THORNTON

Frontispiece: Portrait of Captain Cook engraved by W. Holl from the portrait of Cook by Nathaniel Dance that was commissioned by Joseph Banks in 1776. (*Captain Cook Birthplace Museum*)

First published in 2006 by Tempus Publishing

Reprinted in 2009 by
The History Press
The Mill, Brimscombe Port,
Stroud, Gloucestershire, GL5 2QG
www.thehistorypress.co.uk

Reprinted 2014

British Library Cataloguing in Publication Data.
A catalogue record for this book is available from the British Library.

ISBN 978 0 7524 3995 2

Typesetting and origination by Tempus Publishing Limited.
Printed in Great Britain.

CONTENTS

PREFACE

More than 100 biographies have been written about Captain James Cook since the first was produced nine years after his death by Andrew Kippis in 1788. Few of those biographies have looked in detail at Cook's childhood, the formative years from which the man emerged. Most authors who have described Cook's early years have relied solely on the work of earlier biographers. Few of those who have undertaken original research have escaped incorporating some errors into their work through the misinterpretation of names or dates resulting in errors being compounded in later works. This book is an attempt to correct some of these errors and set the record straight. It has been compiled using early biographies together with information from various histories of the Cleveland area, but more importantly, from a range of original eighteenth-century material largely overlooked by previous writers.

Much of this material does not refer to Cook directly, but to those people with whom he and his family had connections. Examination of his contemporaries in this way has revealed new information about James Cook and gives a fresh insight into his early life.

It is nearly thirty years since I wrote the above words for the first edition of this book. It was then 1978 and 250 years after the birth of James Cook and I thought that all there was to know about him must have been discovered. I have been pleasantly surprised to find that with the passage of time, more Cook material has to come to light, requiring the first edition to be revised and enlarged. One suspects that yet more Cook-related material is still out there waiting to be found and I hope that future researchers will have as much enjoyment in its discovery as I have in recent decades.

Although Whitby lies just outside that geographical area known as Cleveland, I have included references to that town in order to give a fuller picture of the young Cook's connections with the area.

Cliff Thornton
January 2006

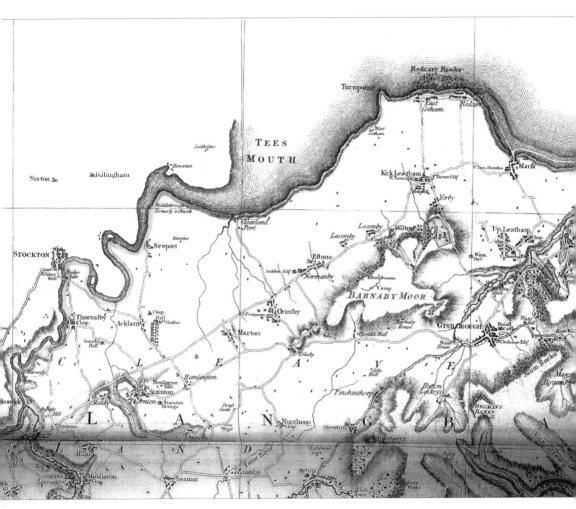

A map of Cleveland in the late 1700s showing the towns and villages connected with James Cook's early years. Note the absence of Middlesbrough. (*Captain Cook Birthplace Museum*)

INTRODUCTION

The story of James Cook's early life is set in eighteenth-century Cleveland, a quiet corner of North Yorkshire. Bounded by the River Tees to the north, the German Ocean (as the North Sea was then called) to the east and the North Yorkshire Moors to the south, Cleveland lay almost isolated from the rest of north-east England. In common with other isolated communities, Cleveland had developed its own customs, legends and dialect.

Most of the population around here lived in the small villages that lay scattered along the green lowlands that bordered the purple heather-covered moors and in the small fishing villages that nestled in the shadow of some of the highest cliffs in England. These villages held close-knit communities that came together regularly on market days and for fairs and religious festivals. In summer, community spirit was particularly important as neighbours co-operated in helping to gather in each others' harvests, for Cleveland's economy was based primarily upon agriculture. Life on the farms was hard, and success depended greatly upon the weather, for this was before the Agricultural Revolution brought the benefits of crop rotation, mechanical implements and improved breeds of farm-stock. Farmers sold their produce (cheese, butter, corn, meat) to local merchants who shipped the goods from ports on the River Tees, like Stockton and Yarm, to London, the vessels returning with manufactured goods and imported luxuries such as sugar, tea and tobacco.

Cleveland society was divided into three levels with the employers (farmers, shopkeepers, craftsmen) over the labouring classes and a landed gentry over them both. This social stratification was usually perpetuated from generation to generation as sons inherited their father's positions in life. It was not until the Industrial Revolution that there were opportunities for improving one's status and although this had already started on Tyneside, fifty miles to the north, it was to be more than 100 years before its effect was felt in Cleveland, with the development of the ironstone mines, ironworks and railways. In the early 1700s the air of Cleveland was still clean and fresh, not yet polluted by the smoke, the smell and the noise of industry. In those days, the rural tranquillity was broken only by the lowing of oxen, or the swish of the scythe, the clattering of a passing stagecoach or the pealing of distant church bells. It was into this peaceful, hard-working, rural society that James Cook was born.

CAPTAIN JAMES COOK, F.R.S.

His FIRST VOYAGE, *performed in His* Majesty's Ship *the* ENDEAVOUR.
SECOND VOYAGE. *The* RESOLUTION & ADVENTURE, *Sloops*
THIRD VOYAGE. *The* RESOLUTION & DISCOVERY.

He was Born at Marton in the North Riding of Yorkshire, And was Unfortunately Killed by the Savages of the Island Owhihee Aged 50 Years & 3 Months.

Portrait of Captain James Cook engraved by Noble from a painting by Wm. Hodges, c. 1784. (*Captain Cook Birthplace Museum*)

I
COOK FAMILY ORIGINS

James Cook was born at Marton, Yorkshire in 1728. He was the second child in the family of James and Grace Cook. His parents had been married three years previously in the neighbouring village of Stainton, when they were thirty-one and twenty-three years old respectively. The register of the parish church still bears, in fading ink, the record of their marriage:

1725 – October 10th   Married James Cook and Grace Pace

Although neither bride nor groom came from the village of Stainton, this was Grace's parish church as her family came from Thornaby, a small village by the River Tees, two miles to the north (see Appendix I for Grace family tree).

In contrast, her husband appears to have had no local connections. He was a Scot and had been born just over the border, in the village of Ednam in Roxbroughshire. He probably had a strict religious upbringing, for according to church records, his father was an elder of the church and would therefore have been responsible for the spiritual and temporal welfare of the parish. The Ednam Kirk Sessions records indicate that his father, John Cook, was a tailor. Unfortunately these are the only known documented facts about the ancestral Cook family, for after the birth of Captain Cook's father, James in 1694, there are no further references to the family in the registers (see Appendix I for Cook family tree).

According to Jeffrey (1859), it is traditionally held that Cook's father moved from Ednam to live in Ayton, Berwickshire, before moving to Cleveland. As the only surviving records for this latter parish commence in the 1740s it has not been possible to substantiate this in any way. However, Kippis (1788) in his biography of Captain Cook, states that his father was supposed to be a Northumbrian from his dialect.

When and why Cook's father came to Cleveland is not known. He was at that time a day labourer going from farm to farm seeking whatever work was available. He was one of thousands of itinerant agricultural workers and of such little social importance at the time that his movements left few footprints in the sands of time.

His first recorded appearance in Cleveland came with his marriage at Stainton in 1725. The earliest biographies of Cook state that his parents lived at Morton

Stainton parish church, where James Cook Snr and Grace Pace were married in 1725. (*Captain Cook Birthplace Museum*)

immediately after their marriage. Morton was not so much a village as an area of rich farmland situated midway between the villages of Ormesby and Great Ayton. Lying within the parish of Ormesby, Morton contained several farmsteads which could have used a willing labourer like James Cook (senior).

A little over a year after their marriage their first child was born. He was baptised at St Cuthbert's church, Ormesby supporting the tradition that they were living in that parish. They named their child John, as it was the name of both their fathers. With his wife's employment opportunities now limited by their baby, James wanted to secure a good job and with this aim the family moved to the nearby village of Marton.

II

MARTON
THE BIRTHPLACE

Monday's child is fair of face,
Tuesday's child is full of grace,
Wednesday's child is full of woe,
Thursday's child has far to go,
Friday's child is loving and giving,
Saturday's child works hard for his living,
But a child that is born on the Sabbath day
Is fair and wise and good and gay.
Anonymous

On Sunday 27 October 1728, Grace Cook presented her husband with their second child. It was a boy and a week later his parents took him to Marton parish church to be christened. He was named after his father and the entry in the baptismal register reads:

No^{br} 3   James ye son of James Cook daylabourer baptized

Few details are known about the circumstances of the family, but all early biographers agree that James Cook was of humble birth. According to Kippis, Cook was born in a mud house. Hutton (1810) gives a more precise description:

..a low cottage, of two rooms, one within the other, the walls of mud, and covered with thatch.

This type of farm labourer's cottage appears to have changed little throughout the eighteenth century, for in 1800, after his inspection of the agriculture of the North Riding of Yorkshire, Tuke (1800) recorded:

The cottages of the labourers are generally small and low, consisting only of one room, and very rarely of two, both of which are level with the ground, and sometimes a step within it. This situation renders them damp, and frequently very unwholesome and

James Cook's baptismal entry in the register of St Cuthbert's church, Marton. (St Cuthbert's church)

A nineteenth-century artist's impression of the cottage in which James Cook was born. (*Captain Cook Birthplace Museum*)

'S.E. view of Marton. The rising hillock is the only remains of the clay-built cottage where Capt. Cook was born', a drawing by George Cuit, *c.* 1788. The remains of the cottage lie in the foreground while the rows of cottages in the distance show the route of Marton Back Lane. (*Wakefield Art Gallery, Ref. Gott 3/36*)

contributes with the smallness of the apartments, to injure the health both of parents and children, for in such contracted hovels numerous families are often compelled to reside.

In 1788, George Cuit, an artist based in Richmond, North Yorkshire was commissioned by Lord Mulgrave to draw various sites in Cleveland associated with Captain Cook's early life. Cuit visited Marton and found that the cottage of Cook's birth had long since collapsed, nevertheless he captured the scene in a drawing that is the earliest known image of Cook's birthplace.

Cuit's drawing also confirms the location of Cook's birthplace, as the cottages shown in the background can be related to the line of cottages shown on a plan of the Marton Estate dated 1764. According to Young (1836), Cook's father was employed as a labourer by Mr Mewburn a local farmer. The plan of the Marton Estate indicates that a Mr George Mewburn occupied a farm just across the road from the Cook cottage.

Despite the availability of work in Marton, James Cook would have been eager to gain better accommodation for his wife and children. Almost anything would have been an improvement on the damp and dirty conditions of their clay biggin. It appears that the family briefly moved back to the parish of Ormesby, as the church register records the baptism of Christiana, the family's third child, in 1731. Being a poor family with few belongings, moving house was not a great problem, indeed many families moved between farms on an annual basis seeking to improve their position with posts offering better terms of employment. It was not long before the Cook family was on the move again, this time back to Marton, where in 1733 Mary, their second daughter, was born.

Both Young (1836) and Ord (1846) stated that the Cooks had lived in two cottages in Marton. It seems reasonable to assume that on their return to the village they moved into a different cottage to the one that young James had been born in. Young (1836) specifies that the family's second cottage was towards the south-west of the village; until the early 1900s there was a field known as 'Cook's Close' in this part of the village.

By now James was five years old and no doubt with his father's enthusiasm for hard work he would have been found plenty of jobs to do both at home and around the village. According to Hutton (1810) he worked in a stable, whilst Ord (1846) stated that he 'tended the stock, took horses for water and ran errands for the [Walker] family', in return for which in the evenings Dame Walker taught him his alphabet and how to read.

Dame Walker is the first of several people who stand out like milestones in Cook's early life. She is mentioned by all biographers and as such has become something of a legendary figure. Unfortunately, as often happens, over the years they have become embellished and exaggerated until it is difficult to distinguish between the fact and the fiction. Coleridge (1852), who believed that Cook's parents paid a few pence weekly for their son's education, saw her as a 'spectacled Tutoress'. In contrast Graves (1808) says that James:

> … as well as the rest of the younger part of the family, was taught to read by the school mistress of the village at an expense which we … can easily suppose did not exceed one shilling per quarter.

Most of these statements seem to be suppositions, or facts passed on by word of mouth several generations after the events have occurred. However, there is at least one contemporary record for Marton in the mid-eighteenth century which appears to have been overlooked by previous historians. This is Archbishop Herring's 'Visitation' in 1743. In April of that year, Thomas Herring had been confirmed as Archbishop of York and in an attempt to determine the state of the Church, he sent out a questionnaire to all clergy in his diocese. From their answers to his questions the Archbishop would determine the temporal and spiritual needs of his different parishes.

One of the questions asked was if there was a school in the parish, and if so, how many children attended. In reply to this question Philip Kitcheon, the Vicar of Marton, wrote:

> There is no school house, a widdow Woman teaches a few small children to read in her own house.

Although this adds little to the legend of Dame Walker, it does negate some of the statements made by Ord who claimed his ancestry from her. He claimed that she was married to William Walker, a respectable yeoman farmer, who lived at Marton Grange and went as far as to record the following memorial inscription from a headstone in Marton churchyard:

> Here lieth the body of William Walker who departed
> this life the 15th day of March 1760 aged 58 years.
> Also Mary, relict of the above William Walker,
> died March 12th 1789, aged 89 years.

As the dates given in this inscription have been confirmed by an examination of the church's burial register, it would appear that Mary Walker was not a 'Widdow Woman' until 1760, long after the vicar's response to Archbishop Herring's Visitation of 1743.

So who was Dame Walker? Sadly we may never know for certain. The church register of Marton parish church records four Walker marriages in the first quarter of the eighteenth century, each one coincidentally resulting in a new Mary Walker for the parish! One of these brides was even described as a schoolmistress at the time of her marriage, so she appears to be the most likely person to have taught James Cook. Entries in the Poor Rate books and minutes of the church council meetings may have shed some light on Dame Walker, but time has taken its toll and these documents no longer exist.

George Cuit, as well as recording the site of Cook's birthplace, also produced a drawing of the schoolhouse at Marton. This drawing shows a woman standing in the doorway of a small, single-storey building, situated on one of the local farms. The plans of the buildings in this farm have been compared with the plans of known farms within the Marton area in an attempt to identify the location of the school, but without success.

By 1736 James and Grace had been married for eleven years, he was over forty years old and no longer as fit or strong as was. With four children to feed and clothe

'School House at Marton' by George Cuit, *c.* 1788. (*Wakefield Art Gallery, Ref. Gott 3/39*)

and maybe more to come, James Cook Snr was seeking a less arduous job that would provide some security for his family. Having lived in and around Marton for over ten years, most local positions that became vacant came to his notice. He knew that there was little chance of finding the job that he wanted locally, so he decided to look further afield.

The early biographers of Captain Cook all agree that the family left Marton in 1736, when young James was eight years old. As James' birthday was in late October this must have meant that the family moved in November or December. These months follow the traditional time of year when agricultural labourers sought new employment. In Cleveland, as in most other parts of the country, these events centred on late October and the Martinmas Hirings. The nearest hiring to Marton was at Stokesley six miles away. There, farmers and labourers would gather when they needed to find their new employees and employers. It was at this annual hiring that James Cook would hope to gain the better position his family needed. He may well have taken his two sons along to show potential employers that although he had reached middle age he had call on two pairs of small but willing hands to do any extra work at no extra cost.

The details of what happened on that day in Stokesley have long been lost to history but the results are known; Cook came home from the hiring having secured the position of hind at Aireyholme Farm, Great Ayton. The farm belonged to Thomas Skottowe, Lord of the Manor of Ayton, although it is unlikely that Skottowe himself would have attended the hiring. Probably Cook met and was actually selected by the tenant farmer at Aireyholme for whom he was to work. Once the terms of his employment had been negotiated, the farmer would have paid Cook the customary 'godspenny' to seal their agreement. Normally this would have been a shilling, or a half-crown if Cook was lucky, paid as a gesture of good faith on the part of the employer to be spent by the worker at the fair which usually attended the hirings. Apart from Christmas and other religious festivals, the few days following the hiring were the only holiday that farm hands could expect in a year, so they usually made the most of it. However, being a canny Scot, and probably teetotal from his strict upbringing, it is likely that the godspenny was used for the benefit of the family, rather than drinking or gambling the money away as many of the men hired that day would have done.

One can imagine Cook, with his two sons, excitedly hurrying home to tell his wife the good news. Over the next few days the family made preparations for their move, packing what few belongings they possessed and visiting friends and neighbours to say their goodbyes. The family was about to make its fourth and farthest move.

Before we follow the family on their move to Ayton we will digress briefly to look at the history of the Marton Estate before the Cooks and we leave it behind. At the time of Cook's birth in 1728, the Marton Estate had just been divided between the five nieces of the previous owner, the late John Lowther of Ackworth Park, near Wakefield, Yorkshire. The estate appears to have been neglected for most of the eighteenth century, being used by the owners merely to provide a source of income from their tenant farmers. However, within thirteen years of the estate being divided up, it was back to individual ownership following the death of one niece and the purchase of land from the others by the fifth niece, Margaret Norton of Sawley.

Following her death in 1774, the estate passed to Sir John Ramsden, her son by her second marriage. In 1786 Sir John sold the manor and estate of Marton to Bartholomew Rudd of Marske. Rudd appears to have been the first owner to take a real interest in the property and started on a programme of developing the village and improving the estate. One of his first actions was to choose a site on which to erect a new mansion. The site that he chose was in the centre of the estate on the crest of a low ridge adjacent to what was then a public highway known as Marton Back Lane. A short distance to the south of the mansion stood the remains of the cottage of Cook's birth. According to Hutton (1810), Rudd was aware of the historical significance of the site of the cottage, for he is reported to have created a memorial at its side. It was nearly sixty years after Cook's birth and the simple clay and thatch construction had collapsed some time before. Rudd eventually had the remains of the cottage removed in order to erect a stable and yard at the rear of his mansion. However, he apparently took steps to ensure that Cook's memory was preserved: it is described in a pamphlet about Cook produced in Whitby in 1837; how he marked out the site of the cottage in his courtyard with a quadrangle of flint stones.

In 1832 Rudd's mansion was destroyed by fire and had fallen into state of disrepair by the time it was bought in 1853 by Henry Bolckow, a leading local industrialist. Bolckow erected an elegant brick mansion on the site of Rudd's old house. Whilst laying out the grounds of his new estate an old workman pointed out the unearthed remains of the site of the Cook's cottage. Bolckow was an appreciative historian and later, in 1858, erected a granite urn marking the site of Cook's birthplace. The urn still stands near the site.

Right: The Cook Memorial Urn, Stewart Park, Marton, Middlesbrough. The inscription reads: 'This granite vase was erected by H.W.F. Bolckow of Marton Hall, AD 1858, to mark the site of the cottage in which Captain James Cook, the World Circumnavigator was born, 27 October 1728'. (*Captain Cook Birthplace Museum*)

Below: Marton Hall before it was destroyed by fire in 1960. (*Captain Cook Birthplace Museum*)

Captain Cook Birthplace Museum, Stewart Park, Marton, opened on 27 October 1978, the 250th anniversary of his birth. (*Captain Cook Birthplace Museum*)

Archaeological investigation of the medieval village of East Marton in Stewart Park, 2003. (*Captain Cook Birthplace Museum*)

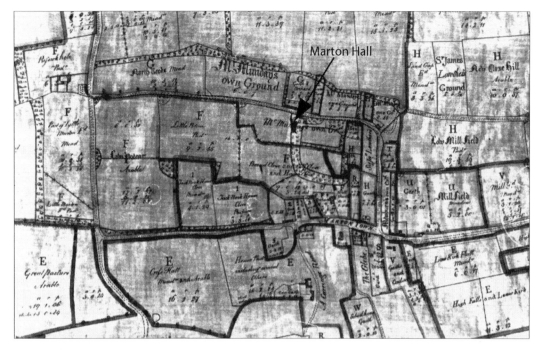

The township of Marton, from 'A Plan of Marton Estate in Cleveland belonging to Sir John Ramsden Bart. by Thos. Forster 1764'. (*Teesside Archives, Ref. U/S/90*)

In 1924 the Marton Estate was bought by Thomas D. Stewart who presented it to the town of Middlesbrough as a public park. In 1960, soon after workmen had started to demolish the hall, history repeated itself and this too was destroyed by fire.

Middlesbrough Borough Council subsequently built the Captain Cook Birthplace Museum on the site of Marton Hall and the new museum was opened to the public on 27 October 1978, commemorating the 250th anniversary of the birth of James Cook.

In 1997 and 2003, archaeological excavations were undertaken in Stewart Park, Middlesbrough, in an attempt to determine whether there were any remains of the birthplace cottage. The results of the excavations suggested that if any remains had once existed they had been lost when the estate was extensively landscaped for Henry Bolckow in the early 1850s (Rowe 1998).

In 1764 Sir John Ramsden, the husband of Margaret Norton, had commissioned a survey of the Marton Estate (see above). This was less than thirty years after the Cooks had lived in Marton and there is no reason to suppose that there had been substantial changes in the tenancies during the intervening years. The plan shows several interesting features relevant to the story of James Cook: fields marked 'G', along the top of the plan, comprise the land farmed by George Mewburn who is said to have employed James Cook Snr.

The farm buildings are situated on the road leaving Marton village, known as Marton Back Lane. On the opposite side of the road is marked the site of the first Marton Hall. As this hall was not built until 1786, it must have been marked upon

Woman spinning in a simple eighteenth-century Yorkshire cottage. (*Costumes of Yorkshire*; a series of watercolours by George Walker, 1814)

the map at a later date. To the right of the hall the plan shows an L-shaped building which may have been the stable block. The approximate site of the cottage in which James Cook was born can therefore be gauged relative to the site of the hall and its stables. Unfortunately no cottage is shown on the plan where one might have expected it to be. This may have been because the surveyor recorded only brick or stone-built dwellings of a permanent nature rather than the temporary clay biggins of the labourers. However, a more likely explanation for the lack of detail in this area is because, according to the plan, the land was designated as 'Mr Munday's own Ground'. This land therefore belonged to Mr Munday and was not part of the Marton Estate that Thomas Forster had been hired to survey. Hence in common with other 'own ground' areas on the plan, details of field names, acreage, usage as well as any buildings, are omitted. Whatever the exact situation of the cottage it can be seen that any dwelling situated in the vicinity of Marton Hall would have been a matter of yards away from Mr Mewburn's farm.

On the lower edge of the plan is a field marked 'W' and named 'Schoolhouse Garth'. Although no building is shown in its vicinity its tenant is listed as Mrs Kitchen who may have been the widow of Philip Kitchen, a previous vicar of Marton parish church.

III

THE FAMILY MOVES TO AYTON

Although only a distance of six miles from their Marton home, the move to Great Ayton had taken the Cook family from the low lands of the Tees Valley up to the sloping hillsides of Roseberry Topping (or Ounesbury Topping as it was then known). Their move also took them through the heart of the village of Great Ayton. It was twice as large as Marton having about 100 families according to information given to Archbishop Herring in his 'Visitation' in 1743. The Cooks would have appreciated the yellow sandstone houses of the village, being far more substantial than the clay cottage that they had started their family in. As they followed the track that ran beside the stream they would have passed Ayton Hall where the Skottowes lived and noted that adjacent to the hall stood the parish church with its bell tower and they would probably have looked with interest at the few village shops.

As the young James would have been told that their farm was just outside the village, he would no doubt have hoped it would not be long before he could return to explore the village. The family would finally have come to the narrow cart track that wound its way up the hillside for 400ft. At the end of the track Aireyholme Farm would have at last come into view as they stopped to catch their breath after the long climb to take a first look at their future home. On their left stood a line of cowsheds built of the local stone and on the distant horizon the conical peak of Roseberry Topping rising to meet the sky.

Aireyholme Farm has remained a working farm over the centuries and is of historic importance in view of the disappearance of so many other places connected with Cook's early life in Cleveland. The farm is still reached via the narrow Aireyholme Lane and the farmhouse still overlooks the main farmyard, although part of the building was expanded in Victorian times. New farm buildings were also added in Victorian times and there is now twice the original length of byres and barns alongside the lane. The haystack built from sheaves of hay shown in Cuit's drawing, has now been replaced by a modern barn containing bales of hay.

Their accommodation was a small stone-built cottage a little to the west of the main farmyard. The precise location of the cottage has been traced thanks to research by members of the Great Ayton Community Archaeology Project. They were guided to the location by information received from the Martin family who had been the tenants of Aireyholme Farm since the mid-1800s.

With this move James Cook had gained the security that he wanted for his family, but the farm, over a mile outside the village, lay in an isolated, exposed position and he may well have hoped that he would not live to regret the move. They had enjoyed a happy and healthy life at Marton and he would be hoping that the next

'S.W. View of Great Ayton' by George Cuit, *c.* 1788. The original parish church, complete with new bell tower (built in Spring 1788) lies on the left of the scene, while in the background the peak of Roseberry Topping rises above the village. (*Wakefield Art Gallery, Re.. Gott 3/42*)

ten years would be as good as the last. Sadly, fate had other plans and death was to become a frequent visitor to the family in the years that followed. It came first to the youngest child, three-year-old Mary. It had been a hard winter and after a long illness she finally died in July of that year. The next day the family walked behind the ox-cart which carried her lifeless little body down to the village where, after a burial service, she was laid to rest in the churchyard.

By the wintertime Grace Cook was with child again. Looking after the family was not as difficult as before, as all the children were now old enough to help about the home. The new baby came in May and was christened Jane (the vicar possibly mistaking her father's pronunciation of 'Jean', the name of her Scottish grandmother). Jane was the first of four children to be added to the Cook family at Ayton. Sadly, however, three of their four new children would die before their fifth birthday.

Despite domestic tragedies life at the farm would have continued as usual and the daily routine of milking the cows and feeding the animals followed regardless. Aireyholme was a mixed farm with cows and sheep grazing on the sloping pastures whilst those fields level enough to be ploughed were used for growing crops. The hired position of Cook at the farm has been described variously as hind, bailiff and head servant. Whatever his position, all biographers agree that his new job would have given him a measure of responsibility in the running of the farm under the

'S.E. View of Airy Holme Farm near Great Ayton' by George Cuit, *c.* 1788. This shows the farm situated on the lower slopes of Roseberry Topping. In the distance on the skyline the artist has depicted the belvedere which still stands and is now known as the Shooting Box. (*Wakefield Art Gallery, Ref. Gott 3/43*)

direction of the farmer who was a tenant of its owner Mr Skottowe.

The Cook family might well have been involved in selling the farm's produce too, taking vegetables, eggs and chickens to local towns on market days and taking cattle and sheep to the annual fairs at Guisborough, Stokesley and Yarm (Tuke, 1800). The October fair at Yarm was particularly important as it was the only cheese fair in the area and attracted people from all over Cleveland. James Cook may have taken his family to this fair and whilst he was busy selling the cheeses, the rest of the family could go and watch the travelling acrobats, jugglers and musicians that entertained the crowds at such fairs (Wardell, 1957).

In addition to attending markets with his father, young James Cook was also a frequent visitor to the village of Great Ayton because he attended school there. It has always been said that it was Thomas Skottowe, the Lord of the Manor of Ayton, who paid for James to go to school and there is no reason to doubt this judging by his subsequent interest and patronage of the young man. Exactly how he came to pay for him to attend school is not known, nor has it been recorded, but there appear to be two possibilities. Firstly, we can be sure that Cook's father knew the value and importance of a good education and would not have wanted the education that James had been receiving at Marton to come to an end. Many workers employed at the annual hirings asked for some sort of payment in kind as well as their weekly pay, and it is possible that in being hired, Cook asked if his son's education could be considered too. Another possibility is that Skottowe being somewhat of a local philanthropist may have noticed James' abilities and decided to sponsor his education accordingly.

The school which James attended was situated in the middle of the village. It had been erected some thirty years previously in 1704 at the expense of Michael Postgate a local yeoman. The school appears to have been successful such that by 1743 the Vicar of Ayton was able to report the following to Archbishop Herring:

> There is one Public School in our Parish: and generally twenty or thirty children are taught in it. Due care is taken to instruct them in the Principles of ye Christian religion according to ye doctrines of ye Church of England: they are duly brought to church as ye Canon requires. *(Ollard and Walker, 1929)*

At Marton, the young James had been taught to read, now at Ayton his education was to continue as he learned the skills of writing and arithmetic, as well as receiving religious instruction. His scholastic achievements do not seem to have indicated that here was a boy of any outstanding ability, although later there was a local story that Cook was so proficient at mathematics he never made a mistake (Heaviside, 1903).

In the early 1800s Graves began compiling a history of Cleveland and appealed in the *Gentlemans Magazine* for any information about Captain Cook's boyhood. He summarised the responses that he received into the following statement:

> During young Cook's continuance at this village seminary it appears that he was never much regarded by the other boys of the school, and was generally left behind in their juvenile excursions; a circumstance, which can only be attributed to his steady adherence to his own plans and schemes, never giving way to the contre-projets of his associates. This, instead of conciliating their regard, naturally rendered them averse from his company. It has been asserted by those who knew him at this early period of his life, that he had such an obstinate and sturdy way of his own, as made him sometimes appear in an unpleasant light; notwithstanding which, there was a something in his manners and deportment, which attracted the reverence and respect of his companions. The seeds of that undaunted resolution and perseverance which afterwards accelerated his progress to immortality, were conspicuous, even in his boyish days. Frequently, on an evening, when assembled together in the village, to set out in search of bird's nests, Cook might be seen in the midst of his comrades, strenuously contending that they should proceed to some particular spot; this he would sometimes do, with such inflexible earnestness, as to be deserted by the greater part of his companions. *(Graves, 1808)*

How long James attended the school is not known, however it is probable that his education continued for some four years, until his twelfth birthday.

After a further three or four years working on the farm at Ayton, the young James was ready to leave home and find a job of his own. He knew that there was more to life than milking cows and ploughing, he had been to markets with his father and visited some of the towns and villages that could be seen from the top of Roseberry Topping. Perhaps he felt the same wanderlust stirring within him that caused his father to leave Scotland so many years before. His father may have sensed

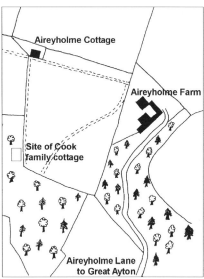

Above left: The site of the schoolroom at Great Ayton as it appeared in the 1940s. (*Captain Cook Birthplace Museum*)

Above right: A plan of part of Aireyholme Farm, Great Ayton showing the location of the cottage where the Cook family lived. (*Great Ayton Community Archaeology Project*)

Aireyholme Farm, *c.* 1905, showing the proportions of the old farmhouse on the right and the expanded accommodation added in Victorian times.

Aireyholme Farm, *c.* 1975. (*Captain Cook Birthplace Museum*)

James' unrest and rather than have him run away from home tried to see if he could help him find a job. His father could not have imagined that when his son did leave home it would be both the first and last time, for although James came to visit his parents in later years, never again did he stay in one place for as long as the eight years that he spent in Great Ayton.

IV

THE CALL OF THE SEA

When sixteen or so years old, James Cook left his home at Ayton farm and started his first job working at Staithes for Mr William Sanderson, a grocer. Within two years he had left Staithes and moved to Whitby to start his sea–going career.

As James Cook was only in Staithes for a relatively short period, most biographers say little more than the above about this stage of his life. And yet this brief period of Cook's life poses a number of fascinating questions, not least, why did he go to Staithes to work in the first place, who was William Sanderson and why did he leave there so quickly?

Staithes is some distance from Cook's home in Great Ayton. If at sixteen James Cook had wanted to work in a shop surely there were opportunities for him that were closer to home; if not in Ayton then in the towns of Stokesley or Guisborough? How could his father have secured him a position at Staithes when his only business contacts were of an agricultural nature? The answer to this question lies not with Cook's father, or his mother (as Fairfax-Blakeborough suggested in 1928), or through the Sanderson family of Ayton as suggested by Besant (1890), but with Thomas Skottowe the Lord of the Manor of Ayton. He had paid for young James to go to school and most probably did not want to see that education wasted by leaving him to became a labourer like his father.

Having recognised that the lad had ability above that of a labourer, Skottowe probably sought to put him to good use, with a chance to improve him further. As Lord of the Manor and a local Justice of the Peace (he attended the North Riding Quarter Sessions from 1735 and sat at Guisborough, Thirsk and Northallerton (Atkinson, 1890)), he would have had the contacts to secure a position for him had he so desired. A note in the diary of Ralph Ward JP actually relates how he had dined with Thomas Skottowe at the Cock Inn and among the constables present was a Mr William Sanderson (Whiting, 1952). Thus Cook's career may have begun in conversation over dinner in a pub in Guisborough. In years to come, Thomas Skottowe and William Sanderson were close friends, their children intermarried with members of the Gill family of Staithes (see Appendix I for family links and Appendix II for the Sanderson memorial) and their sons even sailed together for the East India Company (William Sanderson is listed in the company records as surgeon and Nicholas Skottowe as captain of the *Royal George*) and in his will, Thomas Skottowe

'South view of Guisborough' by George Cuit, c.1788. (*Wakefield Art Gallery, Ref. Gott 3/40*)

nominated Sanderson as one of his trustees. It seems very likely that this was the connection that led to the young Cook securing a job in a shop in nearby Staithes.

William Sanderson is traditionally described in the local histories as a haberdasher and grocer with a shop situated on the seafront overlooking the small harbour at Staithes. He was thirty-four years old when Cook came to Staithes. He had been married for four years and his wife was expecting their second child. It is possible that Sanderson was employing Cook to assist in the shop now that his wife could no longer help.

It was a whole new world for Cook. Compared with the solitude and space of Aireyholme Farm, Staithes was a noisy, busy village cramped into the end of a narrow valley between sea and cliffs. Everywhere he looked he would have experienced new sights and sounds. The scene in Staithes would have been little different when Walter White described it in 1858 as a 'strange town' and recorded his first impression as follows:

> The main street, narrow and painfully ill-paved, bending down to the shore of a small bay; houses showing their backs to the water on one side, on the other hanging thickly on a declivity so steep that many of the roofs touch the ground in the rear: frowsy old houses for the most part, with pantile roofs, or mouldy thatch, from which here and there peep queer little windows. Some of the thatched houses appear as if sunk into the ground, so low are they, and squalid withal. I threaded the narrow alleys and paths

A nineteenth-century print of Staithes. (*Captain Cook Birthplace Museum*)

to look at the backs of the houses from the hill-side. You never saw such queer ins and outs, and holes and corners as there are here. Pigstyes, little back yards, sheds, here and there patches of hill, rough with coarse grass and weeds, and everywhere boat-hooks and oars leaning against the walls, and heaps of floats, tarred bladders, lobster pots and baskets, and nets stretched to dry on open ground above. Imagine besides that the whole place smells of fish and you will have a first impression of Staithes.

The farm boy would have been impressed with the village and his first close encounter with the sea. He had seen it before at a distance from the farm, or rather from the summit of Roseberry Topping, where he could have watched the movements of ships in the 'German Ocean' off the coast of Hartlepool. John Graves in his history of Cleveland (1808) gives a romantic account of this view: 'The River Tees is seen winding through the valley, with stately vessels gliding on its bosom, which give additional beauty'. But here in Staithes Cook, for the first time, could now smell the sea, feel the spray and hear the crash of surf and the incessant cry of gulls as they wheeled overhead.

Sanderson's shop stood on the side of the town's small harbour and the young Cook may have found his attention wandering from his duties to watch the hustle and bustle of life on the harbour-side, watching the boats in the harbour and those passing by further off-shore.

An engraving of Staithes, *c.* 1841

Unfortunately, nothing now remains of the shop where Cook worked. The site is under water some twenty yards offshore, for the sea which provides the livelihood for so many of the coastal villages of North Yorkshire also eats away at the cliffs and sometimes the villages themselves. George Young reported in 1836 that Sanderson's shop had 'long been swept away' although he pointed out that the shop's counter was still in use in another shop in the village. Walter White in 1858 gives a more detailed picture stating that Sanderson's shop and twelve other houses had been washed away during a storm in February 1831. In contrast, Arthur Kitson (1907) reports that the house was dismantled in 1812 for fear of damage by the sea, with most of the materials being used to erect new premises in Church Street. Kitson's account verifies Young's note about the shop counter, although he adds a bit more to the tale by stating that the counter was later moved to Middlesbrough in 1835.

The new premises built in Church Street became known as 'Cook's Shop' and were captured in a painting by Roland Hill in the early 1900s before the shop

Top left: The shop of William Sanderson as rebuilt in Church Street, Staithes. The building is now a private residence known as 'Captain Cook's Cottage'. From a painting by Roland Hill. (*Captain Cook Birthplace Museum*)

Top right: A South Sea Shilling, dated 1723 and bearing the letters 'SSC' denoting that it was made from silver supplied by the South Sea Company.

Above: Shipping off the mouth of the River Tees, from an eighteenth-century view of the Acklam Hall estate by Leonard Knyff. (*Captain Cook Birthplace Museum*)

was converted into a house (Brown and Croden 1977). Hill's painting shows a double-fronted shop with typical eighteenth-century bow windows to either side of a central pair of narrow doors. At the sides of the windows were heavy shutters, needed by all quayside properties as protection from the wind and waves whenever a northerly gale funnelled the sea into the narrow harbour.

Sanderson's traditional description as a haberdasher and grocer greatly undervalues both his role and his status in the local community. Reg Firth (1996 and 1998) has shown that Sanderson was in fact a prosperous merchant. In addition to his shop by the harbour, he owned various properties including a warehouse, houses, a farm and estates totalling several hundred acres.

He was eventually laid to rest in 1773 in the churchyard of the parish church in the nearby village of Hinderwell. As befits a wealthy merchant Sanderson was buried in his family grave capped by a large tombstone bearing a memorial inscription to him, his wife and children (see Appendix II).

It's not clear whether Cook was formally apprenticed to Sanderson or, as George Young described in his *History of Whitby* (1817), after conversations with Sanderson's daughter, he had merely taken Cook on trial, a verbal agreement without any indentures. Either way the young Cook was there to learn the business of shop keeping but with Sanderson's important connections the work would also have provided a potential opportunity for him to enter the world of commerce had he sought this route later. There is some evidence that William Sanderson did in fact take on other apprentices (Thornton, 1997) so there remains a question over Cook's actual terms of employment at the shop.

After eighteen months, Sanderson had probably noticed that Cook's interests lay more with seafaring than work in his shop. Although it would have been an easy matter for Sanderson to rid himself of a disinterested assistant or even to find the lad a place on board one of the small ships that called at Staithes, Sanderson went further than this. We now believe that he went to some trouble to find a suitable outlet for Cook's interests. The fact that he did this might be seen as further evidence of his growing relationship with Skottowe and a subsequent feeling of responsibility for his protégé's welfare.

Although we now feel that Sanderson willingly helped Cook into his next employment there is a story that appeared in some of Cook's earlier biographies that tells an alternative view, one that may have arisen as an attempt to explain the briefness of his stay in Staithes. Kippis, his first biographer (1788), recorded that Cook left after a disagreement with his master and Graves later (1808) claimed that the disagreement was over a lost shilling. Sanderson noticed a shiny new shilling piece was missing from the till and Cook was found to have it in his possession. The master would not believe Cook's explanation that he had replaced it with one of his own coins and accused him of stealing it. As a result of this accusation Cook was said to have absconded the next day and run away to sea.

It is interesting that Young, writing in 1817, and having had contact with Sanderson's daughter, does not mention any disagreement, recording that Sanderson had recognised the youth's preference for a sea-faring profession and had helped him along his way. However, some nineteen years later Young, in his later biography of Cook (1836), provides a detailed account of an altercation between Cook and his master. He records the troublesome coin as being a South Sea Shilling. Such coins were made in 1723 during the reign of George I from silver bullion that had been supplied to the Royal Mint by the South Sea Company. Each coin bore the initials of the company; S.S.C. Young is quick to comment on the significance of the coin's South Sea connection in relation to Cook's future voyages in the Pacific Ocean but it is difficult to believe that after twenty years in circulation such a coin would have remained 'shiny and new'. The story was to evolve still further and by 1891 the shilling was reputed to have contained a hole and therefore traditionally one endowed with good luck – an ideal token for Cook to affix to his watch guard (*History of Great Ayton School*, School Jubilee Committee, 1891). We may assume that like all good stories this one has been elaborated on and modified in the telling and we will probably never know whether there was even a grain of truth in it.

V

APPRENTICE WANTED

We have speculated that as Sanderson probably felt a special responsibility for his young shop assistant through his connections with Skottowe at Great Ayton, it is likely, therefore, that he would have discussed the future of the boy with him and perhaps also with Cook's father. We know that Sanderson made regular business excursions north to Newcastle (the diarist Ralph Jackson records seeing him in the Groat Market on 5 May 1753) and he would perhaps have combined visits to Great Ayton with some of these trips, providing an opportunity to talk about young James' prospects. It is reasonable to imagine, knowing what we now know of his future

exploits, that Cook's interest in the sea was by now considerable – much enhanced probably by his new proximity to it and to the activities related to it in Staithes. He would have talked to sailors that came into Sanderson's shop, those that lived in Staithes and those that were calling in from the colliers that delivered coals to the harbour. Outside he would have talked to the local fishermen as they sat mending their nets on the quayside and perhaps also noticed that sometimes their conversation stopped as he approached them and guessed that he had interrupted smugglers' talk. They would not have trusted a young boy who was a newcomer to the village and especially not one who worked for the son-in-law of the local customs officer!

If, as we assume, discussions had taken place between Sanderson and James' parents and Skottowe it would appear likely that he had agreed to take some trouble to find a suitable placing for him with a reputable local ship-owning company. What was needed was a ship owner who had a good record with his apprentices, one who treated his men fairly, and one whose outlook on life would perhaps not conflict too much with young James' religious upbringing. Sanderson would have known many of the merchants in Whitby but was probably not too familiar with the ship-owners. However he did find out that the Walker brothers, John and Henry, had a good reputation in town. The two brothers were Quakers and as such had acquired a good reputation for fairness and honesty. When Sanderson heard that John Walker was seeking new apprentices, Cook's immediate future would have been as good as sealed.

Once contact had been made with John Walker, the day would soon have come when James would leave Staithes and the world of shop-keeping. Mr Walker would have exchanged letters with Mr Sanderson and James would have gone to Whitby

Fishing cobles drawn up on the beach at Staithes.

Above: 'South East View of Whitby' by George Cuit, *c.* 1788. Among the buildings on the east side of the town can be seen the Methodist chapel which was built in 1788, while Whitby Abbey is shown with the West window which collapsed in 1793. (*Wakefield Art Gallery, Ref. Gott 3/38*)

Opposite: The entrance to Whitby harbour in the early 1800s. (*Captain Cook and Staithes Heritage Centre*)

so that he could meet his potential employer. We might imagine that it did not take James long to gather his personal belongings together and with his master set out on the nine-mile ride to Whitby.

James had probably wondered what Whitby would be like. He would have heard a good deal about it whilst at Staithes, but none of the descriptions that he had been given would have compared with the thrill that he must have felt as he arrived in the town. It must have seemed big – almost ten times the size of Staithes. Whereas the latter village sat alongside the mouth of Roxby Beck, here at Whitby its giant counterpart, the River Esk, ran into the sea both dividing and uniting the two halves of the town that sat on either bank. In place of the squalid cottages and rotting thatches of Staithes, here were handsome terraces of brick and stone, capped by colourful pantile roofs, reflecting the commercial affluence of the town. In the streets people would have moved with an urgency that Cook could not have seen elsewhere. He was witnessing for the first time a town that was not dependant upon the seasons or the turn of the tide for its upkeep.

Cook could not have come to Whitby at a better time, for the town was in the midst of an economic boom. To the north lay the coalmines of Tyneside and Wearside, whilst to the south was London, constantly in need of coal for domestic and industrial use. The ship owners of Whitby had capitalised upon their position situated between the producers and the consumers. The demand for coal from London and elsewhere was met by building more and larger collier vessels to ship the coal from the rivers Tyne and Wear. Whitby shipyards were only too happy to build these additional ships (Whitby-owned ships rose from 113 in 1700 to 260 in 1790). The growth in shipbuilding also benefited a host of allied trades in the town such as rope and sail-making and, last but not least, the increasing numbers of vessels required more and more sailors and apprentices to sail them.

VI
WHITBY AND JOHN WALKER

Who knows what Cook's ambitions were when he entered John Walker's service in 1746? The simple fact that he was going to sea at last may have been his immediate goal, although he may have had his sights set on positions far higher than that of a servant, which is what he was first listed as on the ship's muster rolls. James was to spend nine years in the merchant navy before he joined the Royal Navy in 1755. He spent most of those years in the service of John Walker serving on his Whitby colliers. There is little doubt that the experience and training that he received during this period formed the foundations for his future career in the Royal Navy and his ultimate rise to fame.

Several biographers have reported that little is known of Cook's life during his time in Whitby. (Besant (1910) referred to this period as 'perfectly dark'; McLean (1972) said 'little is known'.) In fact, we now know quite a lot of his activities at this time; whilst the passage of time usually fades the details, the opposite has happened to the story of James Cook. Over the decades more and more information has come to light, until today it is possible to trace Cook's movements more precisely than ever before.

Most of this knowledge of Cook's life in the merchant navy is known thanks to an Act of Parliament, coincidentally passed near the very beginning of his career at sea. In 1747, during the second year of James' apprenticeship, this Act was passed:

> For the relief and support of maimed and disabled seamen, and their widows and children of such as shall be killed, slain, or drowned in the merchant service.

The funds needed to fulfil the aims of the Act were obtained by levying taxes on a ship's crew and the length of voyage which they had made. The easiest way to determine this information was from the ships' muster rolls. Hence, at the end of their voyages, ships' captains had to submit copies of their muster rolls to local tax officials. Although only a minimum of information was needed to calculate the taxes that had to be collected, the early muster rolls listed the following information about each member of the crew:

1. Their name
2. Position on board (i.e. mate, seaman, servant)

3. Age
4. Birthplace
5. Abode
6. Previous ship
7. Date and port where the crewman joined the ship
8. Date and port where the crewman left the ship

Muster rolls are therefore an invaluable source of information both to historians and genealogists in trying to follow the careers of local seamen. In the case of James Cook, his name appears in the muster rolls of four different Whitby ships, in a total of fourteen voyages, as follows:

Freelove, 29th September – 17th December 1747

The earliest record of Cook is as a servant aboard the *Freelove* in 1747. She was a relatively new collier of 341 tons, built at Yarmouth. On Tuesday 29 September 1747, James and nine other apprentices, together with seven other crew had embarked on an eleven-week voyage sailing between the Tyne and London on the East Coast collier run. The voyage ended when the vessel returned to Whitby on Thursday 17 December. Because the new Act requiring the keeping of muster rolls only began in 1747 we cannot confirm the date of Cook's likely first voyage, possibly in 1746. A further complication for biographers trying to identify his first voyage results from the fact that the Gregorian calendar was adopted in Britain in 1752. Prior to that, the new year started in March, so Beaglehole (1974) is wrong when he claims that the first voyage began in February 1747 (see next voyage below) – this was actually the year we would now call 1748.

As the above journey on the *Freelove* began in London we may assume that Cook had made at least one sailing before this, the unrecorded one from Whitby to London.

Freelove, 26th February 1747/8 – 7th June 1748

During the winter of 1747, James would have assisted in overhauling John Walker's ships, preparing them for the next sailing season. After nine weeks the weather had improved and the *Freelove* was ready for the new sailing season. Her crew was very much the same as before with John Jefferson (master), Robert Watson (mate), Thomas Harwood (carpenter) together with James Cook and seven other apprentices who had sailed on the previous voyage. They left Whitby on Friday 26 February 1747/(8), on a voyage that was to last fourteen weeks for the ship, although not so long for Cook. Young (1817) reported that Cook had helped with the rigging and fitting out of a new ship, the *Three Brothers*, under the direction of its owner John Walker. The muster roll entries appear to confirm this story, for on 22 April, after nine weeks at sea the *Freelove* called at Whitby to discharge its mate and five apprentices, including James Cook. Presumably they were all needed to help complete the work on the new ship.

Three Brothers, 14th June 1748 – 14th October 1748

John Walker's new collier was ready to sail on its maiden voyage in early June and left the harbour on Tuesday 14 with Walker himself as master. She was manned by

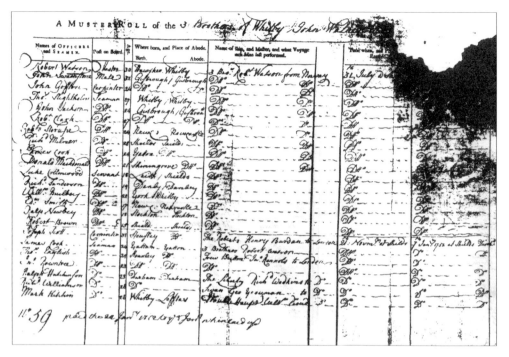

Muster roll for John Walker's collier, *Three Brothers*, from 31 July 1751 to 8 January 1752. James Cook is listed twice as he was one of six seamen discharged at Shields on 28 October, then re-enlisted a month later for the last six weeks of the sailing season. (*Whitby Merchant Seamen's Hospital Houses Trust*)

half a dozen seamen and ten apprentices. After a month at sea, Walker appears to have been satisfied with the vessel's performance and returned to Whitby, the ship's new master, John Jefferson, transferring at sea from the *Freelove*. This maiden voyage lasted only four months. It was the first of four consecutive voyages, spread over eighteen months at sea, that Cook served on board this ship.

Three Brothers, 14th October 1748 – 20th April 1749
Following her maiden voyage, the ship is said to have been hired by the Government as a 'Transport', i.e. transporting troops and supplies. According to Young (1836) the ship was employed taking troops from Middleburg, Holland to Dublin, and later from Dublin to Liverpool.

Three Brothers, 20th April 1749 – 26th September 1749
Cook's third voyage on this vessel was of particular significance for him, for it was during this voyage that his three-year apprenticeship came to an end. His is listed on the muster rolls for the first time as 'seaman' instead of 'servant'. According to Young (1836) during this voyage Cook visited Norway.

Three Brothers, 27th September 1749 – 8th December 1749
Now that Cook had completed his apprenticeship he was no longer tied to the service of Mr Walker, however he remained in his service for one more short voyage

on the *Three Brothers*, until the sailing season was at an end and the ship returned to Whitby for over-wintering. For once Cook did not have to spend the winter helping to overhaul Walker's ships, he was now free to come and go as he pleased. It is possible that he took the opportunity of his newly found freedom to return to Ayton to see his family over Christmas.

Mary, 8th February 1750 – 5th October 1750

After two months leave, Cook decided to exercise his new independence as a seaman and made his way up to the River Tyne for the start of the 1750 sailing season. At the port of Shields he enrolled on the *Mary*, a Whitby collier. The muster roll for this voyage records the ages of the crew. For some reason James Cook's age is given as twenty-six years (he was actually twenty-two) and we are left wondering why he felt the need to add several years to his age!

According to Young (1836) this vessel was employed in the Baltic trade and this is confirmed by the muster roll which bears the name of the Russian port of St Petersburg. After eight months service the ship appears to have been in need of repairs as James Cook and seven other seamen were discharged at London on the 8 October. The ship's carpenter worked on the vessel with the help of the apprentices for eight weeks before the repairs were sufficient to enable William Gaskin, the ship's master, to recruit a replacement crew to sail the *Mary* back to Whitby.

Being discharged in London meant that there were plenty of ships available for Cook to seek employment on. The Whitby muster rolls have not revealed which ship Cook joined, however at the start of the following sailing season Cook's previous ship was listed as the *Hopewell* and his abode is given as Sunderland.

Three Brothers, 19th February 1750/51 – 30th July 1751

For the start of the 1751 season Cook made his way to Whitby again where he joined the crew of his old ship the *Three Brothers*. Maybe after a season working on other ships he now appreciated the conditions on board Mr Walker's ships, or maybe it was the attraction of sailing to foreign parts, for this voyage would take the ship to Norway. The master of the *Three Brothers* was now Robert Watson, who Cook knew, having served under him several times previously when Watson had been mate of the *Freelove* and *Three Brothers*. There was a crew of fifteen under the master: a mate, carpenter and ship's cook, then six seamen and six apprentices. It was a stable crew and there were no changes during the five months voyage. The voyage ended on Tuesday 30 July, but there was to be no leave for the crew as the ship left port on a new voyage the following day.

Three Brothers, 31st July 1751 – 7th January 1752

The muster roll for this voyage shows two entries for James Cook. In the first entry he is listed as residing at Shields. He was one of the fifteen crew sailing under the Master Robert Watson. The ship departed on 31 July 1751 but after only three months at sea the ship docked at Shields where the carpenter and seven seamen were discharged, leaving only the master, mate and six apprentices on board. If the vessel needed repairs it was unusual for the ship's carpenter to be discharged. Nearly a month later on 21 November, a carpenter and six seamen were recruited at Shields, one of whom was James Cook. It appears that Cook may have taken the opportunity of returning home to see his parents, as the second entry on the muster roll lists his abode as Yatton (as Great Ayton was called locally). These latter recruits were discharged at Shields on Tuesday 7 January 1752, and the remaining crew sailed the vessel back to Whitby the following day where she was laid up for the winter.

Friendship, 30th March 1752 – 10th November 1752
The *Friendship* was the fourth Whitby collier on which Cook sailed. His loyalty to John Walker was rewarded with Cook being promoted to his first post as mate, under a new master, Richard Ellerton. The muster rolls show that whilst the voyage lasted just over seven months, only the master, mate and several apprentices remained with the ship throughout. The rolls show a regular discharge and recruitment of crew at her main ports of call Shields, London and Whitby. Returning to Whitby on Friday 10 November, the *Friendship* would have been one of the first ships to be laid up that year. However, that also had the advantage of ensuring that any repairs and refitting could be completed in time for an early start to the sailing season.

Friendship, 2nd February 1753 – 4th February 1754
This was Cook's second voyage as mate, but this time he was serving under a new master, John Swainston. Swainston had also served as mate over Cook on a previous voyage aboard *Three Brothers*. The voyage of the *Friendship* was to last a full year, but as in the previous year, only the master, mate and four apprentices remained with the ship throughout. She returned to Whitby on Monday 4 February 1754.

Friendship, 2nd April 1754 – 28th July 1754
The collier was at Whitby for two months whilst the wear and tear of the previous season were repaired. Whilst Cook retained his position as mate, the master of the vessel had reverted to Richard Ellerton. The short voyage of four months saw numerous changes to the crew before they were all discharged at Shields on Sunday 28 July.

Friendship, 9th August 1754 – 18th December 1754
After discharging her crew at Shields in mid-season, the *Friendship* commenced her collier duties twelve days later having recruited virtually all of the previous crew. The voyage to the end of the sailing season lasted only four months until she returned to Whitby on Wednesday 18 December. Did Cook return to Ayton to see his family for Christmas? It would have been one of his last opportunities for doing so for a long time.

Friendship, 15th February 1755 – 19th July 1755
Allowing the usual two months or so for overhauling the vessels, James Cook returned to Whitby for the start of the new season to find that his friend Richard Ellerton was still master of the *Friendship*. It was Cook's fourth season as mate, but it was also to be his last in Mr Walker's service. Whilst for Ellerton and the *Friendship* the voyage was to last some five months, for Cook it lasted until 14 June 1755. He discharged himself when the ship arrived in the River Thames at Wapping, and three days later presented himself at the Royal Navy's rendezvous for volunteers. After nine years in the merchant navy, Cook's career in the Royal Navy was about to begin.

Is there an explanation for Cook's decision to join the Royal Navy at this time? According to Young (1817) Cook had passed up an opportunity to become master of the *Friendship* in order to join the Navy. It is likely that his decision was premeditated rather than made on the spur of the moment because Walker is said to have supplied Cook with a letter of recommendation to his first captain (Young, 1836). Cook also sought the support of his earlier patrons in subsequent months and as a result both John Walker and Thomas Skottowe wrote to their Member of Parliament, William Osbaldeston, requesting that he in turn write a letter of recommendation to Hugh Palliser, the captain of HMS *Eagle* on which Cook was serving. Palliser evidently recognised the abilities of this new member of his crew and was to become Cook's new patron for his career in the Royal Navy.

VII

THE COLLIER LIFE

Information from the Whitby muster rolls, regarding dates and ports at which seamen were recruited and discharged, together with information from the Newcastle Chamberlain's accounts, indicates that the colliers upon which James Cook served followed a fixed routine. Ships leaving Whitby at the start of a new sailing season first headed fifty miles north to the River Tyne, where they collected their first cargo of coal (there was also collier trade from nearby River Wear). As the only ports mentioned in the muster rolls for those colliers on which Cook served are Shields, Whitby and London, it appears that Walker's vessels only shipped coal from the River Tyne. Arriving at the Tyne within two days of leaving Whitby, a ship would enter only a short distance into the river before anchoring off North Shields. The master would then go ashore and hire a horse to ride the seven miles upstream to Newcastle upon Tyne (Gaskin, 1909).

At Newcastle the master would contact a hostman and negotiate the supply and delivery of coal to the ship, agreeing the type of coal, the quantity and its price. Once an agreement had been reached the hostman would arrange for his keelmen to deliver the coal downstream to the master's ship. Richard Warner, writing in 1802, described the scene as follows:

> The coal is brought down from the works in wagons along rail roads, and poured, by covered wooden channels called staiths (run up at the edge of the river near the works) into boats, or keels as they are here denominated, a clumsy oval vessel, carrying about 20 tons each. These convey the freight to the vessels.

Whilst the master was away in Newcastle, the mate supervised the unloading of the stone ballast from the ship's hold onto the ballast quay. The amount of ballast to be unloaded depended upon the size of the ship. The *Freelove* averaged about 45 tons ballast, whereas the larger *Three Brothers* averaged about 75 tons. By the time the ship's hold had been emptied a loaded keel would be alongside and the dirty job of transferring the coal would begin. The *Freelove* loaded 170 chaldrons of coal (1 chaldron = 36 bushels), whilst the larger *Three Brothers* took onboard 220 chaldrons. There was little rest for the collier crew as the keels were only delayed by the state of the tide or a strike by the wagon men, or the keelmen themselves. (During the 'mini Ice Age' of the mid-eighteenth century the movement of the keels was disrupted when the River Tyne froze over.)

View of Newcastle-upon-Tyne (1783), from the south side of the river, with a coal wagon and keel in the foreground. (*Captain Cook Birthplace Museum*)

Once the coal had been loaded, and the collier was being cleaned of its coating of coal dust, the master returned to Newcastle to pay the taxes that his vessel had incurred. In addition to paying taxes for the amount of ballast that had been discharged and the coal that had been loaded, there was also (from 1732-1763) an additional duty of one halfpenny per chaldron towards the cost of enlarging the pier and harbour at Scarborough (Baker, 1882). Finally, on returning to Shields, the master would recruit seamen needed to make up his crew.

From entering the River Tyne to leaving with the cargo took about one week. The voyage south to the River Thames could be done in just over a week given favourable sailing conditions. However, this sailing time could be extended by several days when vessels were caught in an easterly gale. Harbours along the East Coast were few and far between, and whilst Scarborough harbour had been enlarged to provide shelter for coastal vessels, those unable to make a safe harbour had to risk riding out the storms at sea. Villiers (1967) gives a particularly vivid impression of what life was like under these conditions.

We now know much more about the arrangements for the sale and discharge of coal once the vessels arrived in London thanks to the research of Julia Rae (1997). Cook's marriage, later, to the daughter of a Wapping publican suggests that Walker's ships may have anchored in the vicinity of Execution Dock, Wapping and used the coal heavers of The Bell public house to unload the coal. A gang of sixteen men manhandled the coal into wooden vats on the ship's deck. These vats enabled the volume of coal to be recorded, and taxed accordingly. The coal was tipped from the vats into a lighter moored alongside the collier which transferred the coal to a nearby coal wharf. It was very dirty and dusty work, especially inside the ship's hold, and the landlord would have ensured that his coal heavers received a regular supply of ale to slake their thirst.

Once the ship's hold was empty the collier was loaded up with enough ballast to enable her to sail safely back to the Tyne. The ballast was dredged from the bed of the River Thames and the captain would have to pay ballastage to Trinity House before the ship could depart. The entire process of unloading the coal and taking on the ballast would be completed in about a week. This would give the captain time to undertake any minor repairs to rigging and sails before starting his next voyage.

The ballast taken on by a collier was only a fraction of the weight of coal that it was designed to carry, hence, the journey from the Thames to the Tyne could be made in about a week. Given favourable conditions, a collier could complete a round trip in a little over four weeks. A sailing season from February to November could see up to ten round trips completed. Collier owners then over-wintered their ships in the small harbour at Whitby. This was partly to allow repairs to be undertaken to hulls, sails and rigging but also because owners had to pay a much higher insurance premium for any vessel out at sea between 20 December and 1 March, when the weather was at its worst. The result was that Whitby harbour became a forest of masts during the winter months.

VIII

THE COOK AND
FLECK FAMILIES

In late 1744 when James Cook moved to Staithes, the family that he left behind comprised his parents James and Grace Cook, John his elder brother, sisters Christiana and Margaret, and baby William. Sadly, the ill health that had dogged the family at the Ayton farm persisted and within the next few years both of James' brothers died. When his sister Christiana married a Mr Cocker in the early 1750s, Maragret was left at home helping her parents.

Cook's parents remained at Aireyholme Farm for just over ten years after his departure for Staithes. Then, in June 1755, the same month that his son joined the Royal Navy, James Snr acquired a small plot of land on the outskirts of the village. He had served Thomas Skottowe for nineteen years and in return the Lord of the Manor provided him with a piece of land for his retirement (see Appendix IV). With some help Cook built a stone and brick two-storey cottage on the land. The lintel above the main entrance was engraved with James' and Grace's initials and the date, 1755.

A drawing by George Cuit shows the cottage in about 1788. In the distance of this scene can be seen the peak of Roseberry Topping, whilst to the right can be seen the mill stream that formed the southern boundary of the property. It is thought that Cook Snr subsequently extended the cottage, providing additional accommodation that could be rented out to provide the family with some income.

It was to this new family cottage that James Cook called in July 1757 (Beaglehole, 1974). He was on his way to Leith in the Firth of Forth to join his next ship, the frigate *Solebay*. On 29 June, Cook had been to Trinity House, Deptford, to sit the examination to become a ship's master. He was successful and came away with a certificate that stated that he was qualified, '...to take charge as Master of any of His Majesty's Ships from the Downs thro' the Channel to the Westward and to Lisbon'.

As he made his way north, Cook would surely not have missed the opportunity of spending a few days with his parents. Although he undoubtedly sent them letters describing his exploits while patrolling the approaches to the Channel he would no doubt also have wanted to tell them his news and stories in greater detail. These adventures would pale into insignificance when compared to the voyages of discovery that the future held in store for him.

Within two years he was in Canada helping in the war against France. The fall of

'South East View of a House at Great Ayton which was built by Capt. Cook's Father which House He sold previous to His going to live at Redcar', by George Cuit, *c.* 1788. The stream to the right of the cottage is the mill race referred to in the deed to the land. (*Wakefield Art Gallery, Ref. Gott 3/41*)

The Cook cottage, Great Ayton, prior to 1934 when it was dismantled and shipped to Australia for reconstruction in Fitzroy Gardens, Melbourne. (*Captain Cook Birthplace Museum*)

An early photograph of All Saints church, Great Ayton taken before 1880 when the tower and part of the nave were removed. (*Captain Cook Birthplace Museum*)

Quebec in 1759 was a cause for national rejoicing and in parishes throughout the land the victory was celebrated with the pealing of church bells. The parish church of Great Ayton was no exception and from the church tower its three bells rang out loud and clear over the village (Kettlewell, 1938).

In September 1764, the church bells may have rung out again, this time in celebration of the marriage of Margaret Cook. She was twenty-two years old and went to live in Redcar with her husband, a fisherman of that town, by the name of James Fleck. James and Grace Cook, after forty years of marriage and eight children, were now left by themselves. As if her work in bringing up her children was now complete, Grace Cook died within five months of her daughter's marriage and she was laid to rest in the family grave in Ayton churchyard.

Not much is known about the Fleck family (see Appendix I for Fleck family tree) into which Margaret had married. They appear to have been part of the Redcar fishing community and like many other local fishermen, James Fleck appears to have supplemented his income with a little smuggling.

Smuggling was common along the coast of North Yorkshire and customs officers reported seeing armed cutters laden with contraband goods cruising off the coast waiting for the cobles of local fishermen to bring the goods ashore. Smuggling was so profitable for those involved that there was great resistance to the interference of the customs officers. Smugglers resorted to more and more violence in an attempt to deter the revenue men.

In October 1774, Walter Parks, one of two customs officers responsible for controlling imports along the coast between Coatham and Saltburn, received serious injuries whilst attempting to prevent the landing of contraband at Redcar. To provide protection for the customs officers, in December 1774 a detachment of troops was sent by the Royal North British Dragoons at York to patrol the area. Despite the presence of the troops, violence and threats of violence continued and in December 1775 the customs officers found the following letter on their doorstep:

> Damn you Damn you Ferry and Parks blast your Ise [eyes] you say that you will Exchequer all Redcar but if you do damn my Ise if we don't smash your Brains out … Damn your Ise keep off the sands or else. *(Smith, 1994)*

In early 1776, whilst Captain Cook was preparing for his third voyage, he received a letter from the Guisborough attorney John Harrison. The letter advised him that his brother-in-law James Fleck was accused of smuggling, and sought any assistance that Cook might be able to provide to avoid the accused being taken to court. Cook's first reaction was to seek further information about the charges from the customs officer involved, Walter Parks. Cook had also received a letter from James Fleck himself protesting his innocence. In his reply to Harrison, dated February 1776, Cook hinted that he knew something of his brother-in-law's activities and stated that he could not be of any assistance and recommended that Fleck should try to negotiate with the customs officer in an attempt to avoid going to trial (see letter in Appendix III).

Later, when Margaret and James Fleck were in their sixties and living on a meagre income, one of the local gentry, Bartholomew Rudd, acted on their behalf to try to ease their position. In view of their famous relative he wrote, in 1801, to Sir Joseph Banks asking if he could do anything to help them. Banks first raised the matter with the Admiralty, but they declined to help, and suggested that a public appeal for funds be launched. The plight of the Fleck family was resolved the following year when their situation was brought to the attention of Cook's widow, Elizabeth. She provided the family with an allowance of £20 a year.

Margaret and James Fleck produced a family of eight children, four boys and four girls. Nearly all of their children survived to marry and have children of their own. As none of Captain Cook's children survived, he has no direct descendants, but today there are hundreds of Fleck descendants around the world who are proud of their ancestral relationship to the Cook family (Burnicle and Fleck, 1988). In her will dated 1833, Elizabeth Cook remembered the Fleck family, but as she had outlived both Margaret and James Fleck, she awarded legacies totalling several thousand pounds to their children. Cook himself had left a legacy of £10 to each of his two sisters, Margaret and Christiana.

IX

COOK'S RETURN
TO AYTON

Cook had returned to his home in Mile End Road, London in 1771 following the end of his three-year voyage of discovery in his Whitby-built ship *Endeavour*. He had previously shown his skills in charting the St Lawrence River, and then the coasts of Newfoundland. Now he could add 'navigator', 'astronomer' and 'explorer' to his growing reputation. In the years to come his two further voyages of discovery, in the *Resolution* in the Arctic, Antarctic and Pacific Oceans, would establish Cook as a national hero. There are many existing accounts of these famous voyages and their significance but we continue here now with the account of Cook's associations in Cleveland.

In July 1771, when the *Endeavour* returned to the River Thames having completed her famous voyage, Captain Cook remained in London, finalising his charts of the voyage and preparing for his second expedition. One of his officers, Lieutenant Richard Pickersgill, was granted leave '...to go into the country for the recovery of his health'. Pickersgill left London at the end of September 1771 and, it is assumed, made his way to West Tanfield, near Richmond, Yorkshire, to visit his parents.

On Wednesday 23 October 1771 Pickersgill arrived at Normanby Hall in Cleveland as the guest of Ralph Jackson, member of the local gentry and diarist. Jackson's extensive daily journal records the visit (Teeside Archives). Pickersgill remained there a month, during which time he accompanied Ralph Jackson on a variety of social visits, as well as going out hunting and shooting. On 12 November, Pickersgill visited the village of Great Ayton to attend the sale of the effects of the late Thomas Skottowe who had recently died. It is likely that whilst at the village Jackson introduced him to his brother-in-law Captain William Wilson and it is possible that Pickersgill paid his respects to James Cook Snr as well.

Just over a week later, Pickersgill sailed back to London, courtesy of a sloop that had called into the mouth of the River Tees. Pickersgill returned to his post on the *Scorpion*, the ship that Cook had been temporarily assigned to after his *Endeavour* voyage. Pickersgill returned to find that plans for Cook's second voyage were already underway and the Royal Navy had purchased two more Whitby-built barks. The two ships that had been purchased were the *Marquis of Granby* (450 tons), and the *Marquis of Rockingham* (336 tons). The Royal Navy immediately renamed them as

Above left: William Wilson (1715-1795), Commodore of the East India Company. (*Private collection*)

Above right: Rachel Wilson (1731-1810), sister of Ralph Jackson. (*Private collection*)

Ayton Hall, Great Ayton, where Captain Cook and his wife stayed during their visit to the village in December 1771. (*Dan O'Sullivan*)

the *Drake* and *Raleigh*, and they were sent to the Navy docks at Deptford to be fitted out 'for voyage to remote parts'.

On 29 November 1771 the Admiralty gave orders to Pickersgill to transfer to the *Drake* under Captain Cook. Pickersgill now had the opportunity to tell Cook about his trip to Yorkshire and his visit to Great Ayton. Cook would no doubt have been interested to learn if Pickersgill had met his father and so it is no surprise to find that on 12 December 1771 Cook wrote to the Admiralty requesting three weeks leave, 'Having some business to transact down in Yorkshire as well as to see an Aged Father…'. Cook's request was granted, and a week later he and Elizabeth set off by coach for Yorkshire.

The Cooks did not take their two sons (James and Nathaniel) with them to Yorkshire. Presumably the children stayed at home in Mile End Old Town or were looked after by a neighbour, most likely by Mrs Frances Lieber (*neé* Wardale). She is said to have been a cousin of James Cook and had come down from Yorkshire to live with the family while her husband was away surveying Newfoundland. However, the term 'cousin' was used very loosely in the eighteenth century and no Wardales have been found in the Cook family tree. It is interesting to note though that there was a Wardale family living in Whitby in the late 1700s; Francis Wardale was a solicitor in the town.

The Cooks arrived at the home of William Wilson in Great Ayton on the afternoon of Thursday 26 December. Wilson had been a commodore of the Hon. East India Company's ships until he had retired to Ayton in 1762. His wife Rachel was sister to George Jackson, Deputy Secretary of the Admiralty, and to Ralph Jackson, the Cleveland diarist.

It has long been thought that Captain Cook stayed with his father on this visit to Ayton, but Ralph Jackson's diary records that the Cooks stayed with the Wilsons in the more comfortable surroundings of Ayton Hall. There appears to have been a friendship between the two captains, as in an obituary Wilson is described as being:

> …the early patron and steadfast friend of the illustrious Captain James Cook, between whom and himself a correspondence at once professionally scientific and personally affectionate subsisted during their joint lives. *(Thornton, 1998)*

Mrs Cook was pregnant with their fifth child at the time of their visit and was not a good traveller. She appears to have remained with the Wilsons whilst her husband went visiting family and friends, his first port of call being a visit to his elderly father.

On Sunday 29 December the Cooks would probably have accompanied the Wilsons to All Saints church to attend the weekly service. The church stood adjacent to Ayton Hall, close enough for the families to walk there, and probably also for Cook to pay his respects at the Cook family grave.

Since leaving Whitby, Cook had maintained a friendly correspondence with John Walker. In his letter to John Walker dated 17 August 1771, Cook stated, 'Should I come into the North I shall certainly call upon you…'. On Tuesday 31 December 1771 Cook fulfilled that promise to John Walker, riding a horse over the North Yorkshire Moors to Whitby. Young (1836) relates the story of his arrival

'North East view of Redcar. The Brick House where the Sailor Boy stands was built by Capt. Cook's Father after he left Ayton, tis now occupied by a Sister of Capt. Cooks who is marry'd to Flick, a poor Fisherman', by George Cuit, *c.* 1788. (*Wakefield Art Gallery, Ref. Gott 3/35*)

at the Walkers house in Grape Lane, Whitby when Mary Proud, (John Walker's old housekeeper) overcome with joy at seeing the now famous seaman, threw her arms around him and cried, 'Oh honey James! How glad I is to see thee!'

Cook returned to Ayton two days later, possibly travelling via Redcar to visit his sister Margaret to discuss their father's situation. Their father was seventy-six years old and living on his own. Margaret lived so far away from Great Ayton that she could offer little assistance to her father. The answer appeared to be for their father to sell his property in Great Ayton and move to Redcar to live closer to Margaret. James Cook and his wife left Great Ayton on 4 January 1772 to return to their home in London.

During the next few months James Cook Snr moved to Redcar and temporarily lived with his daughter Margaret whilst a new home was found for him. In May 1771 his property at Ayton was sold and in September of the same year he purchased a plot of land at Redcar (see Appendices V, VI for the deeds). A house was subsequently built for him on this plot of land which was subsequently recorded in a drawing by Cuit in 1788.

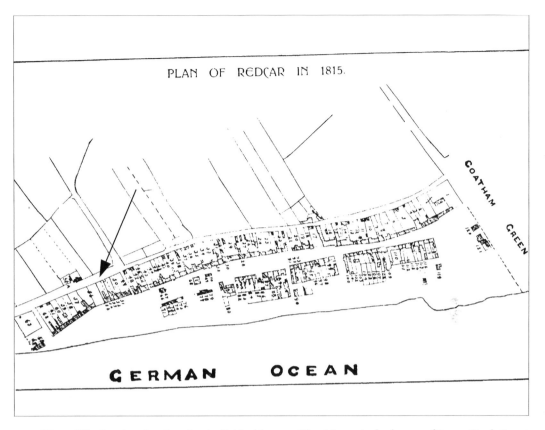

Plan of Redcar in 1815 showing individual houses. Plot No. 55 is the house of James Cook Snr. It stands at the end of a short terrace towards the south end of the town.

It has been possible to identify the location of Cook's father's house using a plan of Redcar drawn in 1815 (above). His house was at the end of a short terrace and appears in the plan numbered as '55'.

Cook's father lived at Redcar until his death in April 1779. He died not knowing that his son had been killed two months earlier in Hawaii. He was buried in the grounds of Marske church since at that time the parish of Marske included the township of Redcar.

X

CONTEMPORARIES WITH CLEVELAND CONNECTIONS

Alexander Dalrymple

Before Cook was appointed to lead the expedition to Tahiti to observe the Transit of Venus in 1769, the Royal Society had already proposed one of their own members, Alexander Dalrymple. The Royal Society was persuaded of Dalrymple's suitability following publication in 1767 of his *Account of Discoveries in the South Pacifick Ocean previous to 1764*. He had written this after twelve years with the East India Company, the latter part devoted to exploration and establishment of the company's trade in the East Indies. However, Sir Edward Hawke, First Lord of the Admiralty, would only agree to a Royal Navy officer commanding a naval ship and Cook got the commission.

Dalrymple had sailed for India in 1752 to take up a clerical post with the East India Company. He sailed on the Indiaman *Suffolk* which was commanded by a certain Captain William Wilson. On arriving in Madras, Wilson took Dalrymple under his wing and looked after him until he was established in his post. This was to be the start of a friendship that lasted throughout their lives.

Wilson's career climaxed several years later with his voyage in the *Pitt* (1758–1760) which established an important new route to China. By this time, Dalrymple had progressed within the company and was taking an interest in trade with the East Indies. It has been suggested that the success of Wilson's voyage in the *Pitt* was in part due to Dalrymple providing the necessary maps and charts of the East Indies (Crowhurst, 1969).

Dalrymple remained in the service of the East India Company for several years after Wilson had retired to Great Ayton in 1762. But on his return to Britain, Dalrymple made sure that he visited his friend. Ralph Jackson recorded in his journal entry for Thursday 12 September 1765:

> While we were breakfasting at Ayton Mr Dalrymple an acquaintance of Br. Wilson in the East India came.

Ralph Jackson (1736-1790),
the Cleveland diarist.

Dalrymple was en route for his family home in Edinburgh and he is thought to have stayed with the Wilsons for a couple of days as the following day Ralph Jackson records Dalrymple joining their hunting party. He again visited the Wilsons on his return journey to London.

It is not known when Wilson's friendship with James Cook began, but there is clearly a possibility that Wilson passed on to Cook the information that he had received from Dalrymple.

Although there are no other records of Dalrymple visiting William Wilson, their friendship remained and twenty years later Wilson asked a favour of Dalrymple. Wilson's eldest son, George, had taken up a post in India with the East India Company and his father wrote to Dalrymple asking if he would kindly write to the senior officer of the company and put in a good word for him to secure a promotion. Dalrymple was pleased to oblige and replied to Wilson:

13th August 1784

Dr Sir,
I shall in a few days by the Cygnet Sloop of war and the Fox packet fulfil your wishes in writing to Mr Russell to be to Your Son what You were to me, and You may be assured nothing could give me more satisfaction that being useful to him...

... a Man who applies himself assiduously to his Publick Duty will in general secure justice to himself and the memory of his Father will always be a recommendation to Your Son.

Omai, the first Polynesian to arrive in England, who visited Cleveland in August 1775.

I believe my occupations will soon allow me to make a visit to the North; but I shall never pass that way without paying my respects at Ayton, I beg my best Compliments to Mrs Wilson.*(Thornton, 2004)*

Joseph Banks and Omai

In July 1774 a bit of the South Seas came to England in the guise of Omai, a Tahitian who had been brought back to England by Captain Furneaux onboard the *Adventure*. Joseph Banks, who had learned a little of the Tahitian language during his voyage on the *Endeavour*, was pleased to take Omai into his care. In the ensuing months Banks introduced Omai to London society and the tall and bronzed Polynesian became a popular figure.

In the summer of 1775 Banks accepted a long-standing invitation from his friend Constantine Phipps to visit him at the family's Yorkshire residence – Mulgrave Castle. Having introduced Omai to the sights and sounds of London, Banks was keen for the Tahitian to see other parts of the country and took him along to visit Phipps. Ralph Jackson, who previously had met Pickersgill and Cook, also met Banks and Omai, recording in his journal for 8 August 1775:

Dined at Mr. Phipps where I saw Mr Banks (who lately sailed round the World) & Omiah a native of Otahite in the S^{O} Seas.

A more detailed account of Banks's visit was recorded by George Colman (1830) who was a youth when he had accompanied the party to Mulgrave Castle. Although written some forty-five years after his visit, Colman recalled many interesting aspects of it, describing how on one occasion whilst out hunting on the Mulgrave Estate Omai was able to catch a partridge with his hands. On another occasion whilst Banks and Phipps excavated a tumulus at the nearby village of Goldsborough, Omai cooked a meal in the traditional Tahitian style; burying the food in a shallow pit which had contained a fire.

Banks also took advantage of his stay at Mulgrave Castle to visit an alum works on the Mulgrave Estate and recorded his visit in a historic manuscript containing a detailed account of the alum manufacturing process. (Thornton, 2000).

Later Colman saw Cook's elderly father in Cleveland. He describes staying several days at Kirkleatham Hall as the guest of Sir Charles Turner and recalls seeing James Cook Snr in the nearby village of Kirkleatham. He had presumably confused Kirkleatham with nearby Redcar but his memory of the meeting makes interesting reading:

His looks were venerable from his great age, and his deportment was above that which is usually found among the lowly inhabitants of a hamlet. How he had acquired this air of superiority over his neighbours it is difficult to say, for his origin must have been humble. His eightieth summer had nearly pass'd away; and, only two or three years previously, he had learn'd to read, that he might gratify a parent's pride and love, by perusing his Son's first voyage round the world! He was the Father of Captain Cook!

XI
COOK MONUMENTS IN CLEVELAND

It is surprising that despite Cook's achievements and fame in his lifetime it was some years before there was a proposal to commemorate his life with a public monument. The first proposal appeared in the *Gentleman's Magazine* in 1787 when a letter to the editor proposed that a commemorative monument be erected in the village of Marton. The writer of this letter followed the tradition of the time of hiding behind a pseudonym, in this case the name 'Cleveland' was used.

Four years later 'Cleveland' again wrote to the editor of the *Gentleman's Magazine*. This time he proposed that Cook be commemorated with a monument erected upon the summit of Roseberry Topping. He indicated that he had been in touch with the landowners and even considered the respective merits of making the monument a column, a tower or a pyramid. He concluded the latter structure to be the most suitable.

In 1811 members of the Stockton Literary Club proposed that a monument be erected to Cook on the summit of Eston Nab. This was some years before the town of Middlesbrough had been established and at that time Stockton-on-Tees was the principle town in the area.

In 1821, a correspondent calling himself 'JB' also wrote a letter to the *Gentleman's Magazine*. He noted that a monument had recently been erected on Eston Nab and suggested that the owner should consider enlarging the structure and naming it in honour of Captain Cook. The elevated site of the location provided an exceptional panorama of the mouth of the River Tees and adjacent coasts, and conversely it would be visible from a large area. The nature of the case made by 'JB' for a monument to Cook resembles so closely that made earlier by 'Cleveland' that one can probably conclude that 'JB' and 'Cleveland' were one and the same person.

So who was this campaigner who had promoted the idea of a Cook monument for over thirty years? The list of members of the Stockton Literary Club who had originally proposed a monument in 1811 included one individual with the initials JB. He was the Revd John Brewster (1754-1842) who had been appointed as curate at Stockton-on-Tees parish church in 1776 and subsequently served in several local parishes. In his spare time Brewster was a keen antiquarian and wrote the *Parochial History and Antiquities of Stockton-on-Tees* (1796).

We can probably conclude that Brewster was the correspondent in which case he must have been delighted with the erection of a large monument to Captain

Above left: Captain Cook
Monument on Easby Moor,
during restoration in 1895.
(*Captain Cook Birthplace Museum*)

Above right: The Revd John
Brewster in 1817, when sixty-three
years of age. (*Captain Cook
Birthplace Museum*)

Right: The Cook Monument
on Easby Moor. (*Mike Kipling
Photography*)

Cook on Easby Moor in 1827. This monument, 51ft tall and built of local sandstone, was erected by the Whitby ship owner Robert Campion. He was the owner of the Easby Estate which contained the moor and he lived occasionally at the nearby Easby Hall.

The monument's height and elevated position unfortunately meant that it was a target for lightning strikes and after sixty years in this exposed position the structure was in a poor state of repair. Robert Campion was by this time dead and the new owner of the estate, J.J. Emerson, declined to bear the full costs of the repair. The local newspaper *The North Eastern Daily Gazette* (forerunner of today's *Evening Gazette*) came to the rescue and launched a public appeal for funds. Sufficient money was found to restore the monument and this time it was fitted with lightning conductors (see Appendix VII for monument's inscription).

In the 1970s and 1980s there was a brief fashion for publishers in the UK to produce illustrated treasure hunt books containing clues to the whereabouts of 'hidden treasures'. In 1982, Hodder and Stoughton published one called *The Piper of Dreams*, basing the treasure hunt on clues relating to Captain Cook. The 'treasure' (a gold, silver and diamond-encrusted flute) was buried close to Cook's Monument. The prize was discovered in 1983.

Great Ayton

There was sadness in the village of Great Ayton in 1933 when the Australian, Russell Grimwade, purchased the Cook family cottage and had it shipped to Australia. It was re-erected in Fitzroy Gardens, Melbourne where it still stands. As some compensation for the loss, Mr Grimwade offered to erect a memorial on the site of the cottage. Just as the cottage had been transported by sea to Australia, he decided that a memorial should be transported from Australia by sea to Great Ayton. It was to be built from granite blocks quarried from Point Hicks (then known as Cape Everard) and was designed as a replica of the obelisk that stood at Point Hicks to mark that part of the Australian coast first sighted by Captain Cook on 20 April 1770.

The stones quarried from Point Hicks were taken to Melbourne where stonemasons fashioned them into the replica obelisk. The blocks were then shipped to England, some of them being packed in the same wooden cases that had brought the cottage from Great Ayton. The blocks were assembled to form the memorial which was officially unveiled on 15 October 1934 – the same day on which Mr Grimwade formally presented the reconstructed Cook cottage to the city of Melbourne.

In 1997 the village received an additional Cook memorial with the unveiling of a life-size statue of the young James Cook. This statue is the work of the sculptor Nicholas Dimbleby and depicts Cook at sixteen years, his age when he left the village and moved to Staithes. The sculpture stands on High Green with Cook orientated towards the distant town of Staithes. The bronze statue was commissioned by Hambleton District Council and was unveiled on 12 May 1997 by Captain Chris Blake, then master of the replica of Cook's ship, HM Bark *Endeavour*, which was visiting Whitby as part of its circumnavigation of Britain.

Above left: The Cook cottage was dismantled and packed into 230 wooden crates. This photograph, taken by Mr Williamson in early 1934, shows the crates loaded onto railway wagons at Great Ayton station, waiting to be taken to Hull docks for shipment to Melbourne.

Above right: The official unveiling of the monument on the site of the Cook cottage at Great Ayton on 15 October 1934. (*Captain Cook Birthplace Museum*)

Right: The statue of the young James Cook at Great Ayton.

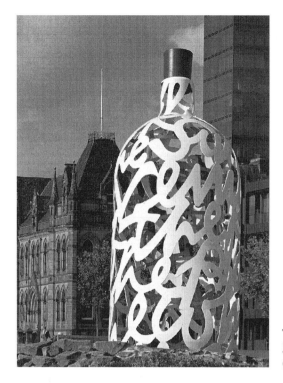

The 'Bottle of Notes' sculpture erected in Middlesbrough town centre in 1993. (*Captain Cook Birthplace Museum*)

A picture postcard from the 1930s showing the statue of Captain James Cook erected on West Cliff, Whitby in 1912. Note the cannon in the distance, a nineteenth-century souvenir of the Crimean War.

Middlesbrough

In 1988 the town's largest public sculpture was commissioned from the artists Claes Oldenburg (Sweden) and Coosje van Bruggen (Holland). They drew their inspiration from Captain Cook and the town's industrial heritage and designed a 35ft tall bottle made from steel, its sides made up of a line taken from Cook's journal from his expedition to Tahiti in 1769:

> We had every advantage we could desire in observing the whole of the Passage of the planet Venus over the Sun's disc.

The sculpture, called the 'Bottle of Notes', was constructed in a disused shipyard on Tyneside. It stands in the Central Gardens near the town centre and was erected at a slight angle, as if the bottle had been washed up on a beach. It was unveiled on 24 September 1993.

Whitby

By far the best known monument to Captain Cook is his life-size statue on the West Cliff at Whitby, overlooking the entrance to the harbour. The story of this monument goes back to 3 November 1908 when *The Times* published a letter from Sir Joseph Carruthers, the recent Premier of New South Wales. In his letter, Sir Joseph commented upon how surprised he had been on his recent visit to London to find that the capital did not contain a single statue commemorating Captain Cook and his many achievements. Sir Joseph's letter pricked the nation's conscience and within months a committee had been established to oversee the creation of a memorial.

By 1910 fund raising was almost complete and the Government had offered a site in the Mall, close to Admiralty Arch. Originally it had been planned to hold a public competition, inviting sculptors to submit proposals for the monument, but it was decided that if this site in the Mall was to be used then design of the memorial should be undertaken by Sir Thomas Brock to complement his other works in that area.

Gervase Beckett, MP for Whitby, was a member of the executive committee overseeing the commissioning of the London memorial and as a keen supporter of the arts, championed the proposal for a public competition. In May 1911, on learning that Sir Thomas Brock was going to undertake the sculpture of Cook, Becket resigned from the committee in protest.

Beckett admired the work of the sculptor John Tweed and immediately commissioned him to undertake a life-size statue of Cook. Beckett subsequently presented the life-sized statue to the town of Whitby and it was unveiled by Lord Charles Beresford on its present site on Wednesday 2 October 1912. It was eighteen months later that Sir Thomas Brock's statue in London was unveiled in June 1914.

Of the two statues, the Whitby statue has proved the more popular both here and abroad. In recent years several replicas have been cast from the Whitby statue and copies now stand at four other locations around the world, most having historical connections with Cook: St Kilda beach, Melbourne, Australia; Resolution Park, Anchorage, Alaska; Victoria, British Columbia, Canada; Waimea, Kauai, Hawaii.

XII

COOK COLLECTIONS
IN CLEVELAND

Before local museums were established, Captain Cook memorabilia was collected by a handful of private individuals in Cleveland. These collectors enjoyed the acquisition and ownership of such material during their lifetimes, but after their deaths their collections were sold, and artefacts that once adorned the walls of their homes were dispersed and are now on exhibition in libraries and museums around the world.

An early collector of Cook memorabilia was Constantine John Phipps (1744-1792). Phipps was educated at Eton College and there made friends with Joseph Banks. While Banks followed an academic career Phipps, at the age of fifteen years, joined the Royal Navy. He worked his way up through the ranks becoming captain in 1765. When he was appointed to HMS *Niger* in 1766, part of a small naval force sent to Newfoundland, he invited Joseph Banks to accompany him on the voyage. Banks collected specimens of the flora and fauna on the expedition as he did later when he accompanied Cook on board the *Endeavour*.

Whilst the two men pursued their separate careers they maintained their friendship through various means including membership of the Royal Society. In January 1776, Phipps inherited his late father's title and became Lord Mulgrave. In the same year he entered Parliament and soon afterwards joined the Admiralty. His experience and interest in the Navy resulted in him developing the finest naval library in England. His library contained first editions of all the publications concerning exploration in the Pacific including Cook's three voyages and those by La Perouse, Bligh and Vancouver.

It was Phipps that commissioned George Cuit of Richmond to draw a series of views of those places in the Cleveland area associated with Cook's early years. These drawings are very large (300mm x 405mm) such that it may have been intended to reproduce them as engravings but no prints of these scenes have been found.

In June 1891, just over 100 years after the death of Phipps, the library at Mulgrave Castle was put up for sale and auctioned by Sotheby's. The most historic item sold was a manuscript copy of Joseph Banks' journal of his voyage on board the *Endeavour* (1768-1771). This was a contemporary copy of Banks' original journal that he had presented to Constantine Phipps. This copy of the journal is now one of the prize exhibits in the Turnbull Library in Wellington, New Zealand.

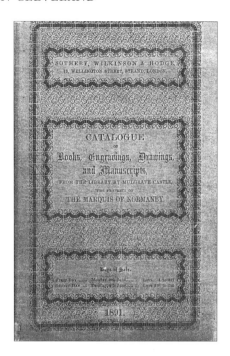

Above left: Portrait of Constantine John Phipps, as Lord Mulgrave.

Above right: Catalogue for the auction of the library at Mulgrave Castle.

Mulgrave Castle, the family seat of Lord Mulgrave.

Above left: Antonino Vella, Keeper of Art at Wakefield Art Gallery, examining one of the drawings by George Cuit.

Above right: Portrait of Henry Bolckow. (*Captain Cook Birthplace Museum*)

It is not known when the portfolio of Cuit drawings was sold, but they were later acquired by John Gott and added to his extensive collection of topographical views of Yorkshire. Following Gott's death, the collection passed through various private hands before being donated to the Wakefield Art Gallery in 1930.

Another prolific collector of Cook items was Henry William Ferdinand Bolckow (1806-1878) a German-born industrialist who came to north-east England in 1827. He had made a small fortune as a corn merchant then went into partnership with John Vaughan to create an iron foundry and engineering works at the new, and still small, town of Middlesbrough.

Bolckow and Vaughan's partnership proved so successful that it soon expanded to include ironstone mines, coalmines and brickfields. As their business grew so did the town of Middlesbrough. In 1853 the town was granted a charter of incorporation by Parliament, and Henry Bolckow was elected its first mayor. As the town grew Bolckow paid for the construction of Albert Park and later the construction of St Hilda's School, and built Marton Hall as his private residence. In 1868 Middlesbrough became a parliamentary constituency and Bolckow was elected first Member of Parliament. He died in 1878 leaving an estate estimated to be worth nearly £800,000. Although Bolckow was a successful industrialist he also had a sense of civic and social responsibility. We have seen that he was responsible for the first marking of Cook's birthplace at Marton (see Chapter 2). Bolckow's interest in Captain Cook, however, extended further than just commissioning a granite vase to be erected in the grounds of his estate to mark the site of Cook's birth. Like most wealthy industrialists Bolckow became a patron

View of Marton Hall from the north. (*Captain Cook Birthplace Museum*)

Interior view of Marton Hall. (*Captain Cook Birthplace Museum*)

THE SALE ROOM

COOK MSS. BOUGHT BY AUSTRALIAN GOVERNMENT

The sale yesterday at Messrs. Sotheby's of the very important manuscripts by, or relating to, Captain James Cook, the explorer, the property of the trustees of the late Mr. H. W. F. Bolckow, M.P., attracted a large number of people, many of whom had probably never before been in these rooms, whilst others had not been there since the days when these rooms constituted the Dore Gallery. At 2.30 the sale of the Powis Library was suspended for a few minutes while the nine lots of Cook MSS. were offered. These MSS. have already been described in *The Times*, and the long-continued suspense as to their ultimate fate is now at an end, for five lots, forming practically the whole of the collection, were purchased by Mr. W .H. Ifould, on behalf of the Australian Commonwealth Government. The collection is intended for the Commonwealth National Library.

The first and most important lot consisted of Captain Cook's autograph MS. of the Diary he kept during his first voyage to the South Seas, May 27, 1768, to July 11, 1771 on 740 pages folio, a MS. of unrivalled interest in the history of Australian discovery. An opening bid of £500 was taken up by Mr. B. D. Maggs and a gentleman not known to the frequenters of Sotheby's, and at £5,000 the lot was knocked down to the stranger in rivalry with Mr. Maggs whose name was revealed when Mr. Ifould sent up his card. The total price paid was £6,780.

Cutting from *The Times,* 22 March 1923, describing the auction of the Bolckow collection of Captain Cook documents.

of the arts and once Marton Hall was completed he began filling its rooms with paintings and objets d'art.

Although we don't know when Bolckow started acquiring Cook memorabilia, we do know that he purchased a portrait of Cook by Webber in 1867 (Stubbs, 1994). His enthusiasm for Cook increased as time went on and he appears to have engaged in an extensive search for items connected with him. By the time of his death in 1878 he had amassed an impressive collection of important documents and artefacts.

When Marton Hall came into the hands of Middlesbrough Borough Council in 1924 it unfortunately no longer contained any of the Cook artefacts. The important Cook manuscripts had been sold by the Bolckow family at Sotheby's in 1923. These included Cook's personal journal of the voyage of the *Endeavour* (1768-1771), the log of the *Endeavour*, a book containing copies of Cook's outgoing correspondence, and a manuscript of Cook's survey of Nova Scotia and Newfoundland from 1762. All of these lots were purchased by the Mitchell Library in Sydney, part of the State Library of New South Wales.

Some items from the Bolckow collection remained in the area; the Webber portrait of Captain Cook was given to Marton parish church in 1934 along with a walking cane said to have belonged to Cook. The portrait hung in Marton vicarage until 1960 when the incumbent, Canon T. Harrison Park, sold it to the Government of New Zealand. It now hangs in the Te Papa, the country's National Museum in Wellington. Unfortunately the whereabouts of the walking cane are no longer known.

John Corner (1823-1890) was also a collector of Cook memorabilia. Born in Whitby, Corner's successful career as a general merchant enabled him to indulge his admiration for Captain Cook through the acquisition of artefacts relating to him. By far the most important item in his collection was the copy of Cook's journal that had been sent back to the Admiralty from Batavia in October 1770. Corner purchased this journal at a Sotheby's auction in July 1890 for the princely sum of £31.

Unfortunately, two months after purchasing the journal, Corner died after a short illness. Before his death he stated his desire to publish the journal and his son

The Bolckow-owned portrait of Captain James Cook by John Webber. (*Captain Cook Birthplace Museum*)

'The Bark, *Earl of Pembroke*, later *Endeavour*, leaving Whitby Harbour in 1768', attributed to Thomas Luny. (*National Library of Australia*)

Marton parish church. (*Captain Cook Birthplace Museum*)

E.E. Anderson standing at the doorway of the West Cliff Art Gallery, Whitby.

ensured that his father's wishes were carried out. The result was the publication in 1893 of the journal under the editorship of Sir W.J.L. Wharton.

Following Corner's death in 1890, his executors sold the original copy of the journal to Australia where it first resided in the Australian Museum and then was transferred to the Mitchell Library in Sydney.

Edward Enoch Anderson (1852-1924), art dealer and artist, started his working life in Whitby as an apprentice to a jet carver. Having served his time in the jet industry he began dealing in fine arts and eventually owned two galleries in Whitby; the West Cliff Art Gallery in Skinner Street and the smaller Rembrandt Art Gallery in Well Close Square. In addition to dealing in fine art he also undertook the restoration of works of art for his clients. He may have been adept at painting too, as in his will his occupation is recorded as 'artist'.

During the summer months when visitors to Whitby were most numerous, Anderson arranged interesting exhibitions of paintings and etchings in his galleries. He also displayed 'a wonderfully interesting collection of Captain Cook's relics'.

Unfortunately the precise nature of these Cook relics was never recorded but it is known that they included a large oil painting depicting a collier leaving the harbour at Whitby. Shortly after Anderson's death, the town's leading auction house was instrumental in arranging the sale of this large painting to the Government of Australia. As the work was neither signed nor dated, Gray, the auctioneer, arranged for several art experts to examine the painting with a view to identifying the artist. The experts agreed that this painting was most probably the work of the British marine artist Thomas Luny (1759-1837) and this attribution was reflected in the valuation of the piece for its sale to Australia.

The painting now hangs in the National Library of Australia in Canberra, where it is now called 'The *Earl of Pembroke* leaving Whitby harbour in 1768'. This painting has become one of the most widely known works attributed to Thomas Luny, although today's art experts suggest that it may not be by this artist after all.

Today the value of items connected with Captain Cook is so great that they can only be afforded by national museums around the world. However, Cleveland is fortunate in having a number of museums devoted to Captain Cook (see Appendix VIII) and all contain some original material relating to Cook, his family, and his voyages of discovery.

XIII

AND FINALLY...

I have often wondered whether Cook had drawn on memories of his Cleveland childhood during his voyages of exploration, particularly when faced with the task of naming the hundreds of new landscape features: mountains, headlands, bays, islands, etc. he saw on his voyages of discovery.

Searches of Cook's journals and charts, however, have failed to reveal any place names in which he incorporated the names Marton, Ayton, Staithes or Whitby. This is not surprising as Cook would have been expected to follow the prevailing naval protocol and name significant features of the landscape after senior figures in the Admiralty, Government, etc.

Captain Cook used only one surname that can be related to a family in Cleveland and that is the name Jackson, used by Cook to name Port Jackson (now known as Sydney Harbour, Australia) and Cape Jackson in New Zealand. These two features were named in honour of George Jackson who was assistant secretary to the Lords Commissioners of the Admiralty at the time of Cook's voyages. George Jackson was from the Jackson family of Richmond, North Yorkshire and was the elder brother to Ralph Jackson the Cleveland diarist.

There is one other place name that links Cook to his home country. In June 1770, the *Endeavour* was slowly making its way north along the coast of Queensland. Cook was charting the coast and assigning names to the various geographical features that he encountered. In his journal for Wednesday 6 June he records the name of a headland as Cape Cleveland. Although his journal does not indicate why he chose to use that name, Beaglehole assumed that Cook had named it after John Cleveland who had been the secretary to the Admiralty from 1751 until his death in 1763 but it seems a bit unlikely that Cook should choose to honour somebody who had died seven years earlier and is much more likely to have been a gesture to the land of his birth.

The headland, which Cook named Cape Cleveland, stands at the eastern end of a large bay, which Cook called Cleveland Bay. To those in authority in the Navy this name would appear to be a natural consequence after the naming of the adjacent cape, but to an ex-farm boy from the north-east, in the eighteenth century, 'Cleveland Bay' would have been more familiar as a local breed of a horse than a long-dead bureaucrat from the Admiralty.

Portrait of Sir George Jackson by Nathaniel Dance. (*Nicholas Ward Jackson*)

Entries in Cook's journal suggest he was keen to name items appropriately, even humorously, an interesting example being his naming of Piercy Island off the coast of the North Island, New Zealand. On 27 November 1769 Cook recorded in his journal that he had named a headland Cape Brett in honour of Rear Admiral Sir Piercy Brett. Cook continued his journal:

> Near one Mile from this is a small high Island or Rock with a hole pierced quite thro' it like the Arch of a Bridge and this was one reason why I gave the Cape the above name because Piercy seem'd very proper for that of the Island.

Whilst Cook strictly adhered to the naval protocol for naming geographical features, his master's mate Richard Pickersgill was less precise. On several occasions, Cook asked Pickersgill to take the ship's boat and undertake a hydrographic survey, or explore to what extent a bay penetrated inland.

Pickersgill had been born and brought up at West Tanfield, a small village two miles north-west of Ripon, North Yorkshire. The charts produced by Pickersgill from his surveys contain features sometimes named after the local wildlife he encountered such as Bream Bay, Mussel Head, Cockel Cove. However, once or twice Pickersgill drew on his memories of northern England when allocating a name. When plotting the coastline east of the Bay of Plenty in New Zealand he called a headland Fair Lee Point and the adjacent bay he named Thirsk Bay (Cobeldick, 2001). Whilst the word 'lee' has a nautical connotation it may also be relevant that it was a surname within the Pickersgill family. It was his mother's maiden name and also the name of his uncle, John Lee, who as a servant of Sir George Jackson is thought to have arranged for him to join the Navy. These names given by Pickersgill have not survived; Fair Lee Point has reverted to its Maori name of Matakaoa Point and Thirsk Bay is now known as Hicks Bay.

Further south along the East Coast of the North Island of New Zealand, Pickersgill assigned the name Duncow Head to a headland. His use of the word 'dun' (an old-fashioned word for grey) is unusual as the cliffs along this coast are white. It may be that Pickersgill called the headland 'Duncow' in memory of the legend of the dun cow associated with the establishment of Durham Cathedral and a name that still can be found on the sign of a number of pubs in the north-east of England. Here again the name given by Pickersgill did not last and it was Cook himself who gave this headland the name by which it is known today – Cape Turnagain.

APPENDIX I

Family Trees

(a) The Pace family of Thornaby (Cook's maternal family).

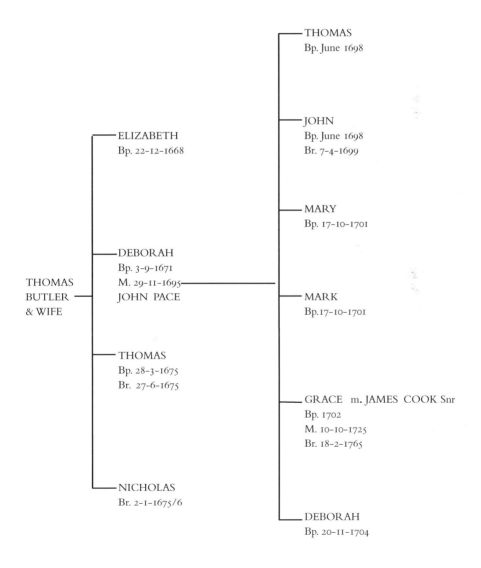

THOMAS
Bp. June 1698

JOHN
Bp. June 1698
Br. 7-4-1699

MARY
Bp. 17-10-1701

ELIZABETH
Bp. 22-12-1668

DEBORAH
Bp. 3-9-1671
M. 29-11-1695
JOHN PACE

MARK
Bp. 17-10-1701

THOMAS
BUTLER
& WIFE

THOMAS
Bp. 28-3-1675
Br. 27-6-1675

GRACE m. JAMES COOK Snr
Bp. 1702
M. 10-10-1725
Br. 18-2-1765

NICHOLAS
Br. 2-1-1675/6

DEBORAH
Bp. 20-11-1704

(b) The Cook family of Marton and Great Ayton (Cook's paternal family).

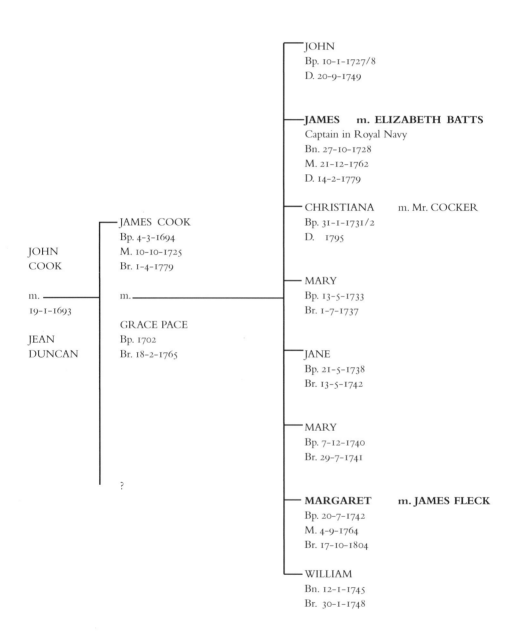

JOHN
COOK

m. ——
19-1-1693

JEAN
DUNCAN

JAMES COOK
Bp. 4-3-1694
M. 10-10-1725
Br. 1-4-1779

m. ——

GRACE PACE
Bp. 1702
Br. 18-2-1765

?

JOHN
Bp. 10-1-1727/8
D. 20-9-1749

JAMES   m. ELIZABETH BATTS
Captain in Royal Navy
Bn. 27-10-1728
M. 21-12-1762
D. 14-2-1779

CHRISTIANA   m. Mr. COCKER
Bp. 31-1-1731/2
D.   1795

MARY
Bp. 13-5-1733
Br. 1-7-1737

JANE
Bp. 21-5-1738
Br. 13-5-1742

MARY
Bp. 7-12-1740
Br. 29-7-1741

MARGARET   m. JAMES FLECK
Bp. 20-7-1742
M. 4-9-1764
Br. 17-10-1804

WILLIAM
Bn. 12-1-1745
Br. 30-1-1748

(c) The Fleck family of Redcar (Cook's in-laws through his sister).

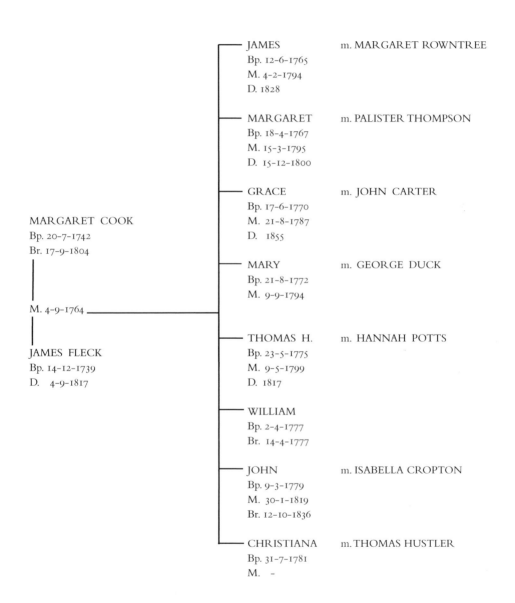

MARGARET COOK
Bp. 20-7-1742
Br. 17-9-1804

M. 4-9-1764

JAMES FLECK
Bp. 14-12-1739
D.   4-9-1817

JAMES   m. MARGARET ROWNTREE
Bp. 12-6-1765
M. 4-2-1794
D. 1828

MARGARET   m. PALISTER THOMPSON
Bp. 18-4-1767
M. 15-3-1795
D. 15-12-1800

GRACE   m. JOHN CARTER
Bp. 17-6-1770
M. 21-8-1787
D. 1855

MARY   m. GEORGE DUCK
Bp. 21-8-1772
M. 9-9-1794

THOMAS H.   m. HANNAH POTTS
Bp. 23-5-1775
M. 9-5-1799
D. 1817

WILLIAM
Bp. 2-4-1777
Br. 14-4-1777

JOHN   m. ISABELLA CROPTON
Bp. 9-3-1779
M. 30-1-1819
Br. 12-10-1836

CHRISTIANA   m. THOMAS HUSTLER
Bp. 31-7-1781
M. -

(d) The Skottowe family of Great Ayton (Cook's childhood benefactor).

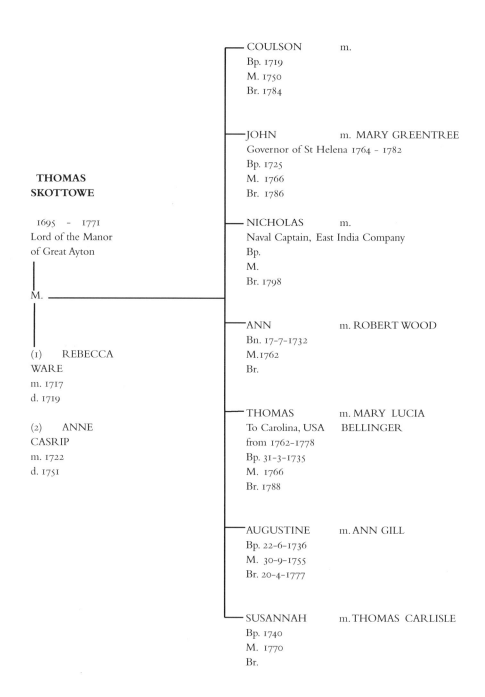

**THOMAS
SKOTTOWE**

1695 – 1771
Lord of the Manor
of Great Ayton

M.

(1)   REBECCA
WARE
m. 1717
d. 1719

(2)   ANNE
CASRIP
m. 1722
d. 1751

COULSON   m.
Bp. 1719
M. 1750
Br. 1784

JOHN   m. MARY GREENTREE
Governor of St Helena 1764 – 1782
Bp. 1725
M. 1766
Br. 1786

NICHOLAS   m.
Naval Captain, East India Company
Bp.
M.
Br. 1798

ANN   m. ROBERT WOOD
Bn. 17-7-1732
M.1762
Br.

THOMAS   m. MARY LUCIA
To Carolina, USA   BELLINGER
from 1762-1778
Bp. 31-3-1735
M. 1766
Br. 1788

AUGUSTINE   m. ANN GILL
Bp. 22-6-1736
M. 30-9-1755
Br. 20-4-1777

SUSANNAH   m. THOMAS CARLISLE
Bp. 1740
M. 1770
Br.

(e) The Skottowe – Sanderson relationship (Cook's benefactor and first employer)

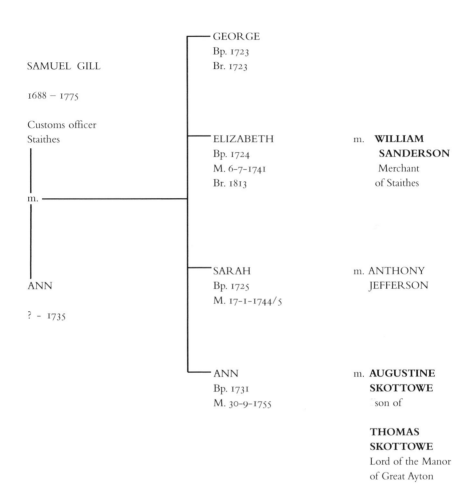

SAMUEL GILL

1688 – 1775

Customs officer
Staithes

m.

ANN

? – 1735

GEORGE
Bp. 1723
Br. 1723

ELIZABETH
Bp. 1724
M. 6-7-1741
Br. 1813

m. **WILLIAM
SANDERSON**
Merchant
of Staithes

SARAH
Bp. 1725
M. 17-1-1744/5

m. ANTHONY
JEFFERSON

ANN
Bp. 1731
M. 30-9-1755

m. **AUGUSTINE
SKOTTOWE**
son of

**THOMAS
SKOTTOWE**
Lord of the Manor
of Great Ayton

Appendix II

Memorial inscription on the Sanderson family tomb, Hinderwell parish churchyard.

South Face:

To the memory of WILLIAM SANDERSON of Staithes
Merchant, who died Nov. 12th 1773 aged 62 years,
and ELIZABETH his wife who died Dec.-1813 aged 89 years.
THOMAS their son died in the East Indies aged - years
ISAAC their son died Dec. - 1801 aged 30 years
AUGUSTINE their son died April 19th 1819 aged 57 years

North Face:

To the memory of the children of William
and ELIZABETH SANDERSON -

SAMUEL who died at Durham	April 7th 1752 aged 10 years
WILLIAM in the East Indies	April 1767 aged 22 years
ISAAC	May 24th 1753 aged 5 years
SARAH	Nov. 20th 1757 aged 6 months
JAMES	Sept. 15th 1758 aged 10 days

All these 3 last are interred near this tomb

ROBERT	Oct. - aged 21 years
WILLIAM	Sept aged 19 years

Top Face:

Also JOHN SANDERSON who died July - 1832 aged 81 years
Also ELIZABETH daughter of WILLIAM and ELIZABETH SANDERSON
and wife of THOMAS RICHARDSON
of Manchester who died August 1813 aged 63 years.

The grave of William Sanderson and family in Hinderwell parish churchyard.

APPENDIX III

Letter from Captain Cook regarding his brother-in-law's alleged smuggling activities.

Jn. Harrison Esq, Attorney at Law, Guisbrough

Mile End, London 24th Feb. 1776

Sir,

I have had some conversation with Mr Parks, on the subject of the letter which you favoured me with. He seem to think, that my Brother in Law, James Flick, cannot know neither the time nor place he Run the good(s) for which he stands charged; as the officers of the Customs are very carefull to conceal these particulars. If so, he cannot know himself to be innocent, unless he never was concerned in such work; and this I suppose is not the Case. Consequently he will in my opinion run no little risk in standing a Trial. But this is a subject I have little knowledge of, Nor have I time nor inclination to make my self acquainted with it. I am told that the easiest way to get clear of such like affairs, is, after the Writ is served, to Petition the Commissioners of the Customs and Excise, to which it may belong; and to endeavour to make up the matter with the officers concerned. If this method is pursued, I shall be ready to give any assistance in my power, which cannot be much, as I know not a single Commissioners at either the one Board or the other. This Method or proceeding supposes him Guilty the contrary of which he has not only asserted to you but to me also in a letter which I have just received. The only thing he seems to dread is the expence of a Trial, but in this I wish he does not deceive himself, as well as you. If I should gain any further information you shall be acquainted therewith...

This letter is held in the National Library of Australia, Canberra. Manuscript reference MS 7.

APPENDIX IV

Indenture for James Cook Snr's acquisition of land at Great Ayton, 1755.

A Memorial of an Indenture Tripartite bearing date the 16th Day of June, in the 28th year of the reign of our sovereign Lord King George the Second, in the year of our Lord 1755, made between Thomas Skottowe of Great Ayton in Cleveland in the County of York, Esquire, of the first part, Ralph Ward of Guisborough in the County of York, Gentleman of the second part and James Coke of Great Ayton aforesaid Yeoman, of the third part, of and concerning all that piece or parcel of waste ground lying and being within the town of Great Ayton aforesaid as the same is now marked and set out containing in length 22 yds. and 2 ft. or thereabouts, in breadth at the south end thereof 10 yds. or thereabouts and at the north end thereof 12 yds. or thereabouts and adjoining on a close or parcel of ground called Hollygarth towards the east, the mill race towards the south, and on the common or waste ground towards the west and north. The sd. Indre. (indenture) as to the Extion (execution) thereof by the sd. Thos. Skottowe is witnessed by

Wm. Lawson of Stokesley in the sd. County of York, Gentleman and Thos. Wrightson of Great Ayton afd. (aforesaid) gardiner and as to the Extion. thereof by the sd. Ralph Ward is witnessed by Margt. Peirson of Guisbrough afd. Spinster, servant to the sd. Ralph Ward and the sd. William Lawson. Signed and sealed by the sd. James Cook in the presence of William Lawson, Thomas Wrightson.

North Yorkshire County Records Office, Deed No. Z124–176.

APPENDIX V

Deed of Sale for James Cook Snr's cottage and land at Great Ayton, 1772.

A Memorial of an Indenture Tripartite bearing date the 16th Day of May, in the year of our Lord 1772, made between James Cooke late of Great Ayton in the County of York and now of Redcar aforesaid, yeoman, of the first part, and Thomas Pennitt of Great Ayton aforesaid, gentleman, of the second part, and Charles Jackson of Great Ayton aforesaid, yeoman of the third part, concerning all those two several cottages, dwelling houses or tenements with the garth or parcel of ground to the same belonging and adjoining containing in whole length 22yds. 2 ft. and in breadth at the south end 10yds. And at the northern end 12 yds. And all that hedge or fence of the said Thos. Pennitt 20yds. Or so lying between the said garth and the lands of Thos. Pennitt, which premises are bounded by the lands of Thos. Pennitt towards the east, the Mill Race towards the south and on the Townstreet towards the west and north, property now in the occupation of Ann Morley and the said Charles Jackson and the said James Cooke or their undertenants.

Signed by James Cooke
Witnessed by John Mathews of Stokesley.

North Yorkshire County Record Office, Deed No. BC 21–35.

APPENDIX VI

Indenture for James Cook Snr's purchase of land at Redcar, 1772.

A Memorial of an indenture bearing date the Twenty Sixth day of September in the Year of our Lord 1772 made between the Right Honorable Sir Lawrence Dundas of Aske Hall in the County of York, Baronet, of the one part and James Cooke of Redcar in Cleveland he said county, Yeoman of the other part, and Concerning all that piece or parcell of Ground as the same (was) marked and set out Containing

Eight Yards in Breadth and Forty yards or thereabouts in Length, situate, lying or being within the Town, Township or Territory of Redcar aforesaid in County of York adjoining on the Lands of Ralph Agar towards the East, on a parcel of (land) recently sold by the said Sir Lawrence Dundas to Richard Lincoln the Younger towards the West, on the Townstreet of Redcar aforesaid towards the North, and on a Lane or Common Highway called the Back Lane otherwise Garth End Lane towards the South, and now in the Occupation of the said James Cooke his undertenants or Assignees with the appurtenances, which said Indenture as to the Execution thereof by the said Sir Lawrence Dundas is Witnessed by John Craneford servant late of Aske Hall aforesaid Gentleman and William Williams of the same place servant to the said Sir Lawrence Dundas – and as to the Execution thereof by the said James Cooke Witnessed by Bartholomew Rudd and John Harrison both of Guisborough in the sd. County Gentlemen.

Signed and sealed} Bartw. Rudd
In the presence of us} John Harrison & Sworn James Cooke

This extract from the deed kindly provided by Vera Robinson of Redcar.

Appendix VII

Inscription on the Cook Monument on Easby Moor.

In memory of the celebrated circumnavigator Captain James Cook FRS A man of nautical knowledge, inferior to none, in zeal prudence and energy, superior to most. Regardless of danger he opened an intercourse with the Friendly Isles and other parts of the Southern Hemisphere. He was born at Marton Oct. 27th 1728 and massacred at Owythee Feb. 14th 1779 to the inexpressible grief of his countrymen. While the art of navigation shall be cultivated among men, whilst the spirit of enterprise, commerce and philanthropy shall animate the sons of Britain, while it shall be deemed the honour of a Christian Nation to spread civilisation and the blessings of the Christian faith among pagan and savage tribes, so long will the name of Captain Cook stand out amongst the most celebrated and most admired benefactors of the human race.

As a token of respect for and admiration of that great man, this monument was erected by Robert Campion Esqr. of Whitby AD 1827.

By permission of the owner of Easby Estate J.J. Emerson Esqr. it was restored in 1895 by the readers of the *North Eastern Daily Gazette*.

APPENDIX VIII

Captain Cook-related museums and resources in Cleveland.

Great Ayton:
Captain Cook Schoolroom Museum
101 High Street
Great Ayton
North Yorkshire
TS9 6NB
Tel: 01642-724296
www.captaincookschoolroommuseum.co.uk

Middlesbrough:
Captain Cook Birthplace Museum
Stewart Park
Marton
Middlesbrough
TS7 6AS
Tel: 01642-11211
www.captcook-ne.co.uk/ccbm/index.htm

Staithes:
Captain Cook and Staithes Heritage Centre
High Street
Staithes
TS13 5BQ
Tel: 01947-841454

Stockton on Tees:
HM Bark Endeavour
Castlegate Quay
Moat Street
Stockton on Tees
TS18 3AZ
Tel: 01642 676844
www.castlegatequay.co.uk

Whitby:
Captain Cook Memorial Museum
Grape Lane
Whitby
North Yorkshire
YO22 4BA
Tel: 01947 601900
www.cookmuseumwhitby.co.uk

Whitby Museum
Pannett Park
Whitby
YO21 1RE
Tel: 01947 602908
www.durain.demon.co.uk

Useful websites:
Captain James Cook (1728-1779)
www.captcook-ne.co.uk/ccne/index.htm

The Captain Cook Tourist Association
www.captaincook.org.uk

The Great Ayton Community Archaeology
   Project
www.historic-cleveland.co.uk

The Captain Cook Society
www.captaincooksociety.com

BIBLIOGRAPHY

Anonymous, 1837.
Captain Cook the Circumnavigator (Whitby pamphlet).

Archbold, William Arthur Jobson, 1900.
George Jackson – entry in *Dictionary of National Biography*.

Atkinson, John Christopher (Editor), 1890
The North Riding Record Society for the publication of original documents relating to the North Riding of the County of York.
Quarter Sessions Records, Volume 8.

Baker, J.B., 1882.
The History of Scarborough.

Beaglehole, John Cawte, 1968
The Journals of Captain James Cook on his voyages of discovery.
Volume 1. *The Voyage of the Endeavour 1768-71*.

Beaglehole, John Cawte, 1974.
The Life of Captain Cook.

Besant, Sir Walter, 1890.
Captain Cook.

Brown, Jane and Croden, Ian, 1977.
Staithes.

Burnicle, Ada and Fleck, Rod, 1988.
A Genealogical Study of the Family of Captain James Cook RN, FRS, 1728-1779.

Cobeldick, Trevor, 2001
Cook Voyage Place Names of New Zealand.

Coleridge, Hartley, 1852.
Lives of Northern Worthies.

Colman, George, 1830.
Random Records.

Craster, H.H.E., 1907.
A History of Northumberland. Volume III
The Parish of Tynemouth.

Crowhurst, R.P., 1969.
The voyage of the Pitt – a turning point in East India navigation.
Mariner's Mirror Vol. 55, pp.43–56.

Dixon, Joyce, 1996.
History under the Hammer.

Fairfax-Blakeborough, John, 1928.
Captain James Cook. An Historical Play to celebrate a Great Yorkshireman and benefactor of the Empire.

Firth, Reg, 1996.
William Sanderson of Staithes.
Cook's Log Vol. 19, No. 1, p. 1227.

Firth, Reg, 1998.
William Sanderson – haberdasher and grocer.
Cook's Log Vol. 21, No. 2, p. 1494.

Gaskin, Robert Tate, 1909.
The Old Seaport of Whitby.

Gott, Ron, 1968.
Henry Bolckow, Founder of Teesside.

Graves, John, 1808.
The History of Cleveland in the North Riding of the County of York.

Heavisides, S,M., 1903.
Rambles in Cleveland.

Hutton, William, 1810.
A Trip to Coatham in Yorkshire.

Jeffrey, Alexander, 1859.
The History and Antiquities of Roxburghshire and adjacent districts, from the most remote period to the present time.

Kettlewell, Robert Mountjoy, 1938.
Cleveland Village. Being notes …on some of the records of Great Ayton.

Kippis, Andrew, 1788.
The Life of Captain James Cook.

Kitson, Arthur, 1907.
Captain James Cook.

Maclean, Alistair, 1972.
Captain Cook.

McCutcheon, K.L., 1939.
Yorkshire Fairs and Markets.
Publications of the Thoresby Society, Volume XXXIX.

Ollard, Sidney Leslie, and Walker, Phillip Charles, 1929. (Eds)
Archbishop Herring's Visitation Returns, Vols I, II, III.
Yorkshire Archaeological Society, Record Series Volume LXXII.

Ord, John Walker, 1846.
The History and Antiquities of Cleveland.

Rae, Julia, 1997.
Captain James Cook Endeavours.

Rowe, Peter, 1998.
The archaeology of East Marton: Captain Cook's Birthplace.
A report by the Tees Archaeology Unit.

Skottowe, Philip F., 1963.
The Leaf and the Tree.

Smith, Graham, 1994.
Smuggling in Yorkshire 1700-1850.

Stubbs, Ian, 1994
Henry Bolckow (1806-1878)
Cook's Log, Vol.17, No.3, pp.1046-1049.

Thornton, Cliff, 1997.
The Diary of Ralph Jackson (1736-1790). Part III: William Sanderson of Staithes.
Cook's Log, Vol.20, No.3, pp.1410-1411.

Thornton, Cliff, 1997.
Wakefield's Captain Cook watercolours.
Cook's Log, Vol.20, No.4, pp. 1448-1449.

Thornton, Cliff, 1998.
The Diary of Ralph Jackson (1736-1790). Part IV: Commodore Wilson of Great Ayton.
Cook's Log, Vol.21, No.2, pp.1496-7.

Thornton, Clifford E., 2000.
Sir Joseph Banks's account of alum making at Kettleness, North Yorkshire.
The Cleveland Industrial Archaeologist No. 26, pp.13-18.

BIBLIOGRAPHY

Thornton, Cliff, 2004.
Commodore Wilson's Archives.
Cook's Log, Vol.27, No.3, pp.43-44.

Tuke, John, 1800.
General View of the Agriculture of the North Riding of Yorkshire.

Villiers, Alan, 1967.
Captain Cook, the Seaman's Seaman.

Wardell, John Wilford, 1957.
A History of Yarm.

Warner, Richard, 1802.
A Tour through the Northern Counties of England and the Borders of Scotland.

Whellan, T. and Company, 1859.
History and Topography of the City of York and the North Riding of Yorkshire.
Vol. II.

White, Walter, 1858.
A Month in Yorkshire.

Whiting, Charles Edwin, 1952 (Ed).
Two Yorkshire Diaries (Ralph Ward's Journal).
Yorkshire Archaeological Society. Record Series Vol. CXVII.

Young, George, 1817.
The History of Whitby and Streoneshalh Abbey. Vol. II.

Young, George, 1836.
The Life and the Voyages of Captain James Cook.

ACKNOWLEDGEMENTS

I must thank Phil Philo and John Robson for first highlighting the need for a revised edition of this book and then pestering me into actually doing something about it.

I am most grateful to Phil Philo of The Captain Cook Birthplace Museum for his encouragement and his assistance in providing many of the images used to illustrate this book.

I am also grateful to those many individuals and organisations that have kindly allowed me to reproduce illustrations and documents in their possession, particularly:

Antonino Vella of the Wakefield Art Gallery
Reg Firth, Captain Cook and Staithes Heritage Centre
David Tyrell of Teesside Archives
The Revd Mike Proctor of Marton parish church
The Trustees of the Whitby Merchant Seamen's Hospital Houses
Dan O'Sullivan and the Great Ayton Community Archaeology Project
Vera Robinson of Redcar
The National Library of Australia
Nicholas Ward Jackson

Many members of the Captain Cook Society have provided me with practical assistance and encouragement throughout this project; I greatly appreciate their enthusiasm and support.

INDEX